Disarming
the Culture War

Disarming
the Culture War

✦

How the Silent Majority
Can Break the Stalemate

Bruce Wilson

iUniverse, Inc.
New York Lincoln Shanghai

Disarming the Culture War
How the Silent Majority Can Break the Stalemate

iUniverse books may be ordered through booksellers or by contacting:

iUniverse
2021 Pine Lake Road, Suite 100
Lincoln, NE 68512
www.iuniverse.com
1-800-Authors (1-800-288-4677)

ISBN-13: 978-0-595-37932-3 (pbk)
ISBN-13: 978-0-595-82303-1 (ebk)
ISBN-10: 0-595-37932-X (pbk)
ISBN-10: 0-595-82303-3 (ebk)

Printed in the United States of America

Contents

Preface vii

Culture War 1

An Alternative 11

Abortion 22

    When Does Life Begin 33

    It's My Body 51

    Unwanted and Defective Birth 63

    Everybody's Doing It 69

Guns 76

    The Second Amendment Myth 83

    The Protection Dilemma 91

    Guns Don't Kill 99

    Curbing a Violent Culture 106

Separation of Church and State 115

    In God We Trust 122

    School Prayer 132

    In or Of the Public Square 138

Church and Citizen 145

Gay Marriage 154

Pandora's Box 161

Enough Already 173

Disarming 178

Preface

Though I have long had both a desire to write and a deep interest in the moral issues of our day, any pursuit of these interests was rightfully placed on the back burner many years ago. Such interests were relegated to the lower levels of a priority list that has been dominated by an even stronger desire and interest in properly providing for and raising a family of six children. "Struggling author" and "adequate provider" seemed to be incompatible objectives, so I concentrated on the latter, knowing that priorities would quite naturally change someday. Someday arrived in November of 2004 as my wife and I, recent early retirees, watched election returns in our empty nest, as our six adult children likely watched the same coverage in their own homes and apartments many miles away. As I flipped from channel to channel to hear commentator after commentator express utter amazement that exit polls identified moral values as the preeminent election issue—the one issue that certainly determined that the United States would be led for the next four years by President Bush and not President Kerry—I determined that it was time to pursue the personal interests that had long been simmering on the back burner.

It was a relatively easy process to decide on the format for this book. The sections of the book follow a natural progression through each of the main issues of the Culture War—abortion, gun control, separation of church and state and same-sex marriage. These sections are sandwiched between an introduction to the Culture War and a concluding chapter with recommendations on how concerned citizens can become active participants in the effort to move beyond this divisive stalemate.

The content of this book was also easy to determine. I have felt for many years that hard-core Republicans and Democrats have hijacked their respective party platforms and staked out inflexible positions on these moral issues that do not represent the true sentiments of the majority of Americans. I know for certain that the two major parties do not represent my positions on these issues. I also believe it is clear from the many polls that have been taken concerning these issues that I am far from alone. One of the primary objectives of this book is to show that the stalemate of the Culture War is the product of our two political parties and not the product of an equally divided country. There is no doubt that serious division exists on these four issues, but the nearly equal division that was made manifest in the two most recent presidential elections is not an accurate representation of how the entire electorate feels about these issues. I believe this book will more than adequately make that case.

As a first time author, I readily acknowledge that my credentials will be a significant hurdle to overcome in attracting readers to this book. It would of course be an easier sell if I were an author with an already established media platform or an academic background that seemed relevant to the topic. My reply to any such concerns is to strongly emphasize that this is not an academic topic. As citizens, each of us is expected to reach our own conclusions on the four moral issues of the Culture War. Text books and professors are not consulted as ordinary citizens determine for themselves where they stand on abortion, gun control, gay marriage and separation of church and state. The conclusions reached are quite often based on faith, emotion or intuition and not necessarily supported by a comprehensive logical framework. The success of political commentary is at least partially based on the author's ability to articulate clearly what his or her audience might already believe but has not had the time or desire to fully articulate. The author is essentially providing a framework of thought for an existing but, perhaps, incomplete belief. In this book, I believe that I have developed a logical and common sense articulation of what many others are already thinking on this subject. The proof of such an assertion can only be determined by readers who pass judgment on the ideas and the manner in which they are expressed herein.

Clearly not every reader will agree with the conclusions reached in this book. These are difficult and divisive issues. I will consider this a success if like-minded readers appreciate the common sense framework that can perhaps supplement and support already existing views, and if readers who disagree with the conclusions are motivated to explore their own opinions to more fully understand why we disagree. A more rational dialogue would be good for both sides. Finally, if there are any readers whose opinions on these issues are still malleable, it would be a great privilege to have influenced them to the point of taking a stand, one way or the other.

I have learned through this process that though writing is a solitary pursuit most of the time, it must not be all of the time. I am extremely grateful to my family for their encouragement and practical support throughout. All six children and my wife Mary have provided valuable feedback, most of which has made its way into the material that follows. I have to single out Matthew for his political insights and knowledge, Kevin and his wife Wendy for taking the time to review many drafts and especially Christopher for serving as the editor. His professional training and skills improved my original drafts immeasurably. I, of course, am responsible for any shortcomings and mistakes that exist.

Culture War

In the aftermath of President Bush's narrow and arguably unexpected re-election in November of 2004, journalists and commentators from all points on the political spectrum have flooded the media with revelations of a starkly divided America. If you spent even a small amount of time viewing any of the cable or network news programs in the weeks and months following the election, you are certainly very familiar with the graphical representation of red and blue America that has become a ubiquitous symbol of a divided nation. By now, most of us are quite comfortable using red and blue labels to describe political orientation. We all likely know whether we live in a red or blue state, if our particular city or neighborhood is a blue or red zone, and perhaps even know the "political color" of each of our friends and neighbors. Even though Jay Leno could likely locate several exceptions right outside his studio, most of us would be hard pressed to identify an acquaintance who doesn't know that "red" equals conservative and Republican and "blue" equals liberal and Democrat.

Because of the intensity of the current media attention, this red and blue phenomenon may seem to be a product of this most recent election, but it's not. The current configuration of red and blue states is nearly identical to the electoral outcome of the previous presidential election. It was truly a new phenomenon then, but its relevance and importance were lost in the wake of the political fallout from the election. The post-election analysis in 2000 focused on Florida, recounts, lawyers and courts, leaving little time for consideration of the implications of the red and blue divide. Thankfully, President Bush's re-election in November didn't end in another recount fiasco, and the post election attention squarely focused on understanding the differences between red and blue voters. Now, with the hindsight of two consecutive elections exposing the red and blue divide, it's clearly an important and significant trend that cannot be ignored. Both major political parties and an army of political analysts are intensely focused on understanding the basis of this political fragmentation.

It's not surprising that significant energy and financial resources are expended by political organizations to understand why a person ultimately voted red or blue. After all, political success is measured in votes. Understanding what motivates and persuades voters is the life-blood of a political party. But it isn't just the professionals who are interested in this topic. The curiosity shown by ordinarily non-political Americans is very surprising. Usually at the end of a long election process, we are weary from the constant, repetitive campaigning and the endless "expert" analysis that accompanies it. Presidential elections seem to go on forever. We look forward to election day, not just for the opportunity to express our opinion, but also as an opportunity to "give the hook" to a political show that has dragged on too long and lost the interest of its audience.

But this time around there is no rush to put it behind us. Red versus blue is a primary topic of conversation around the proverbial water coolers of America. Interest in the postmortem political analysis is unusually high. Why? I think it primarily has to do with the fact that a plausible and understandable explanation for the division between red and blue was immediately available as the polls closed on November 4th. Everyone within earshot of a television or radio heard nationwide exit poll results that found voters identified "moral values" as the most important campaign issue. Even more astounding, fully 80 percent of those who rated moral values as the number one issue voted for President Bush:

Most Important Issue	All Voters	Voted For Bush	Voted For Kerry	Voted For Other
Moral Values	*28%*	*80%*	*18%*	*1%*
Economy/Jobs	20%	18%	80%	0%
Terrorism	19%	86%	14%	0%
Iraq	15%	26%	73%	0%
Health Care	8%	23%	77%	0%
Taxes	5%	57%	43%	0%
Education	4%	26%	73%	0%

—Presidential Election National Exit Poll 2004 CNN

In the midst of a global war on terror, bogged down in a difficult and increasingly unpopular war in Iraq, and at the same time struggling to come out of a moderate recession, it was surprising to find that moral values was a primary factor in the outcome of the election. Commentators and analysts seemed more stunned than surprised. It's quite remarkable that so many Americans based their vote primarily on moral issues. In every past wartime election, the issues of war and economic performance have dominated the factors determining the outcome of the election. To find moral values leading the list of election issues is so out of the ordinary that there have been attempts to discount the impact, especially by Democrats. In an effort to mask the importance of an issue that weighed so heavily against them, Democrats prefer re-arranging the list by grouping the two war related issues together as one category, and the economic and welfare issues together in a second category, thus demoting moral values to third place on the list. As much as Democrats would like the issue to disappear, manipulating the polling data is not going to change the fact that moral values was not just a significant issue—it was the decisive issue. If moral values had not been of primary importance to so many red voters, the outcome of the election would have been reversed. It was the deciding factor for President Bush and, therefore, is the key to understanding the red and blue divide.

I believe this topic has captured the attention of the nation precisely because moral values are at the heart of what divides America. I think we are beginning to realize that differences between red and blue voters are not related to political policy, they are related to fundamental values. This is a significant distinction. Ordinarily, Americans might disagree on "how" things ought to be accomplished—the policy—but not the value of "why" something should be accomplished. For example, nearly all Americans share the value of providing security for the elderly. Some favor the policy represented by the existing social security system, while others favor a different policy that would modify social security to include private accounts. Though the policies are different, the value of providing security for the elderly is the same. These policies represent two different ways of accomplishing the same goal. For the most part, politics has been the process by which we debate and select from differing policies in order to accomplish common goals.

For most of our history, an overwhelming majority of Americans have shared common values and as a result, have shared common goals. I have heard it said before that America is not just a state; America is a state of mind. It's a clever phrase that conveys a very profound truth. America is likely the only nation in the history of the world founded primarily on ideas and values, not on geographic proximity, common language or conquest. American values are the glue that binds us together as a nation. It's not surprising that such unity of purpose has existed so long. After all, for most of our history, America has been a nation of immigrants who came here primarily because they believed in American values and wanted the opportunity to live those values. Common values were not imposed, they were acquired by choice. Because a significant majority of Americans have always shared the same fundamental values, political disagreements over policy have been easily tolerated. We have always had different opinions on how things should be accomplished, but not why they should be pursued. The shock of the last two elections is that we no longer have such unity of purpose. We are no longer just debating policy. We are now debating core values and guiding principles. No wonder it has captured our attention. Questioning American values is the equivalent of questioning the very foundation of our society.

As this issue has been dissected by pollsters and analysts, a general consensus has been reached that four underlying issues are the source of the divide:

- Abortion

- Gun Control

- Separation of Church and State

- Gay Marriage

Though these issues seem to have burst on the political scene just recently, the roots of this moral divide were firmly planted in the decade of the 1960s, as a variety of challenges to traditional American moral values were raised in public debate, and perhaps more importantly, in the courts. Anyone who lived through the '60s will recognize that the re-evaluation of sexual morality in that decade was a precursor to both the abortion and gay marriage issues that we face today. Likewise, the secularist movement of the '60s laid the groundwork for the current debate over the separation of church and state. The values divide might seem to have come upon us quickly, but it has been simmering beneath the surface for 40 years.

The official "fork in the road," the point at which red and blue paths began to diverge, was engineered by the Supreme Court in early 1973 with the Roe v. Wade decision that legalized abortion. This one decision, and the rapid widespread implementation of legal abortion that followed, is without doubt the primary source of the rift that has developed between red and blue. Those who would later be identified as red voters proceeded forward on one fork of the road, while future blue voters proceeded forward on the other. As with most forks in the road, the initial separation of the two paths was not great. But over time the distance between the two has become painfully noticeable. This separation has been further exacerbated by court and legislative decisions over the last 40 years that seemed to favor secularism over religion to the great dismay of red voters.

As Americans, we are well known for our unique ability to focus completely on the road ahead instead of dwelling on the road already traveled. Occasionally an out of the ordinary event will cause us to turn around and reflect on the path we have traveled to reach our current destination. It can be an eye opening experience. It's very possible that one recent event is responsible for opening our eyes to the significant degree of separation between the two diverging paths of red and blue. The event occurred last year when the mayor of San Francisco joined the state Supreme Court of Massachusetts in legalizing gay marriage, challenging yet another traditional value. Taken alone as a moral issue, I doubt gay marriage itself would have generated such an outpouring of opposition. However, when added to the existing list of moral issues separating red and blue, it appears to have been the "straw that broke the camel's back," exposing the divergent paths we have been on for quite some time. Whether or not gay marriage was truly the final straw isn't really important. What is important is that the separation is now so complete and widely recognized, that we have even developed a short-hand title to describe it—Culture War.

If either the red or the blue side held a significant advantage in the Culture War, this issue would not generate the level of interest that it is now receiving. At first glance, the national map of red and blue states is deceiving. If you look at the raw number of red states and the extensive geography they occupy, you might conclude that this is a war the red side is clearly winning. The map is a vast sea of red except for two little islands of blue floating on opposite coasts. But in general, the red states are more rural and less densely populated than the blue states, which are home to the nation's largest cities and have highly concentrated populations. In terms of voter support, red and blue are about as equally balanced as can be. The two are separated by such a narrow margin, that President Bush actually lost the popular vote in 2000, and won by a margin of less than 2 percent in 2004.

It's this small margin of separation between red and blue that forces the two major political parties to mine the polls for data that will allow them to better understand what can be done to attract voters of the opposite persuasion. The margin is so narrow that even a small swing in one direction or the other can mean the difference between winning—or losing—a Presidential election. If Democrats and Republicans stick with the current party platforms on these four moral issues, we will continue to be a deeply divided nation. Neither party's platform will attract a significant majority of the electorate. And meaningful change by either party seems unlikely. Republicans have no incentive to change. They were victorious in both rounds of voting in the Culture War, and even saw an increase in their margin of victory the second time around. There are some minor rumblings of fielding a presidential candidate in 2008 who has more moderate views on the cultural issues in the hope that this candidate could draw some blue voters away from the Democrats. But the majority view in the Republican Party is to continue with more of the same. It's difficult to avoid such complacency in the afterglow of two consecutive victories.

Democrats, on the other hand, are of necessity in the midst of some serious soul searching. Not only did the Democrats lose the White House in this election, but they also lost a number of seats in both the Senate and the House. They lost so many seats that they are now the minority party in every branch of government. It's the first time since the election of 1928 that the Republicans have controlled all the levers of government at the same time. The downward slide has the Democrats running scared. How scared? Consider the following statements from the most unlikely source, Hillary Clinton, made on January 24th, 2005:

> "Yes, we do have deeply held differences of opinion about the issue of abortion, and I for one respect those who believe with all their hearts and minds that there are no circumstances under which any abortion should ever be available," the former first lady said.

> "There is an opportunity for people of good faith to find common ground in this debate. We should be able to agree that we want every child born in this country to be wanted, cherished and loved," she added.

> "We can all recognize that abortion in many ways represents a sad, even tragic choice to many, many women," Clinton said. "The fact is that the best way to reduce the number of abortions is to reduce the number of unwanted pregnancies in the first place."

> —as quoted by Marc Humbert, Associated Press Writer, Jan 25, 2005

Who would have ever believed that Hillary Clinton, previously recognized as one of the most steadfast supporters of abortion, would show such sympathy for the red, anti-abortion point of view? And she isn't the only Democrat who's showing a red side:

> Still recovering from their crushing losses on Nov. 2, Senate Democrats today will turn to Harry M. Reid (Nev.), a quiet insider and consensus-builder, to succeed Thomas A. Daschle (S.D.) as their minority leader.

> Reid, a Mormon from tiny Searchlight, Nev., lacks Daschle's flair as a speaker and public figure and rarely goes on TV outside his home state. Moreover, he gets along well with Republican leaders and has parted company with most Democratic lawmakers on some prominent issues, such as his support for a constitu-

tional ban on flag burning and his opposition to abortion in most cases.

—Charles Babington, Washington Post Staff Writer, Tuesday, November 16, 2004

Democrats in the Senate didn't just turn to Senator Reid to lead them; they also turned their backs on a pro-abortion party platform that has been costing them votes. Reid wouldn't have had a snowball's chance in Searchlight, Nevada of obtaining this post except for the fact that his anti-abortion credentials make him a useful reminder to red voters that not all Democrats toe the party line

Over the course of the next four years, we will see many other Democrats reposition themselves as either open minded sympathizers or as outright supporters of red values. I don't believe that any of these convenient political transformations will result in a significant shift in levels of support for either party. A leopard can change its spots, but it's still a leopard. Voters are not fooled that easily. In fact, they often turn on candidates and parties that show an inability to stand firm on principle. It is possible to shift the balance of power slightly with a more conservative candidate on the Democratic side or a more moderate candidate on the Republican side. But one way or the other, it's highly likely we will continue to be a deeply divided country—either slightly Democrat or slightly Republican—unable to find a significant governing majority.

A heart-felt, convincing platform change from either party on the moral issues could shift the balance of power substantially. Unfortunately, current party platforms are so deeply entrenched, that revision of party orthodoxy on these issues is nearly impossible. Platform positions and candidates for office are selected by extremely dedicated and committed party members, not the general public. The party faithful are not about to give up the faith. These moral issues have become defining principles for both parties and outright change is not open for discussion. Both parties will tolerate some chipping around the edges, but the foundation will not be destroyed.

It's not just the political party structure that perpetuates the stalemate in this Culture War. Meaningful public discussion of any of these four moral issues is now almost impossible. Instead of dialogue, we have monologue. Each side is armed to the teeth with talking points and verbal slogans. Yet this abundance of talk has left each side unable or unwilling to listen. Compounding the problem, most of us are extremely uncomfortable even talking about these issues. We might have very strong feelings about the issues, but feelings are difficult to articulate and even more difficult to turn into logical, convincing arguments. There is also the further complication that for many of us, these are religious issues that aren't to be debated but to be taken on faith. For these reasons, discussion is eagerly avoided at every opportunity. Why talk about something so contentious and difficult to express? It's much easier just to avoid it.

It might be easier in the short term, but the lack of constructive dialogue on these moral issues is one of the primary reasons we find ourselves in a Culture War that has deeply divided the country. Shared, common values have always been the foundation of American culture, and now with that foundation weakening considerably, I think there is a growing desire in the country to do something about the widening gulf between red and blue. As I've already pointed out, I don't think constructive dialogue will be initiated by the two major political parties. It's my hope the comments that follow will add to the public dialogue—a dialogue that is necessary if we are to find our way beyond this Culture War.

An Alternative

The American political process can be a lot like a voluntary "tug of war" competition. Most of us have had some experience with this game. A referee brings out a long sturdy rope, lays it on the ground and marks a victory line in the ground at the center of the length of rope. Two teams of volunteers line up at opposite ends of the rope. Every member of each team grabs hold of the rope on their side of the dividing line and prepares to use the rope to pull the opposing team across the center line. The referee gives the signal for the game to begin, engaging both sides in a struggle to pull the other team over the line. Sometimes, one team is strong enough to make short work of the game as the weaker team soon tumbles over the center line. But other times, the teams are equally matched and locked in a stand-off. At this point, it is not uncommon for spectators who have been observing from the sidelines to join one team or the other in an effort to provide relief to the struggling participants and bring an end to the game. Whether they are caught up in the excitement, or just want the game to end, many join in with one side or the other. Eventually one side prevails and drags the weaker team over the line.

It isn't very often that one of the two teams in our political "tug of war", Democrats or Republicans, has sufficient strength to pull the other team across the victory line without the additional help of the spectators who initially prefer to stay on the sidelines and not join either team. In fact, in the Culture War each of the two major political parties, Democrat and Republican, can only count on roughly one-third of the population to be strongly committed to the party and its candidates. To win elections, one party needs to attract more voters than its opponent from the remaining one-third of the voting population that is either independent or only "leaning" to one party or the other. The precise size of each of these three groups is of course debatable and even fluctuates over time. The size of the "persuadable middle" could be more or less than one-third of the population, but there is no doubt that at the present time and for the foreseeable future, it's large enough to deny either party a clear-cut majority.

This group of voters in the middle has often been referred to as the "silent majority." I don't think there has ever been a more appropriate political label. It perfectly describes the status of voters who are not committed to either major political party. In relative terms, this group is "silent" in comparison with the two political parties. They have no political organization and therefore no ability to combine their voices in a common message, as the political parties are able to do. Because they have defined platforms, well scripted positions, and skilled, articulate spokespeople, the two parties are the source of nearly all political discourse that makes its way into the mass media. The voices of Democrats and Republicans saturate the airwaves and countless lines of print reflect their dialogue, but the "voice" of the middle is seldom, if ever, heard through the same mass communication channels. A cynic might conclude that the media have a vested interest in preserving the voice of the two political parties and stifling the voice of the silent majority. It's true that the media certainly benefits from pitting Democrats against Republicans. One-on-one battles produce better theater than those between three combatants and ratings are surely better when the two sides are engaged in verbal combat. But I don't believe that we ought to be cynical in seeking explanations for the silence in the middle. Even if the silent majority were given the opportunity to speak out, who would speak and what would they say? There is no organization to develop and project a common voice. It's just a fact of life that in a two party political system, there is only room for two voices, not three.

Just as the word "silent" is a perfectly descriptive component in the silent majority label, the word "majority" fittingly describes the inherent political power of this group. While the silent majority itself doesn't constitute an electoral majority, neither political party can reach majority status without attracting votes from this group. Republicans and Democrats alike will always be short of a majority unless they attract a sufficient number of voters from the unaffiliated middle to lift them over the 50 percent hurdle. This necessity to attract votes from the silent majority is the reason party strategists are always talking about candidates "moving to the middle" during a general election campaign. During primary elections, where only the party faithful can be counted on to vote, Democratic candidates emphasize liberal issues and Republican candidates emphasize conservative issues because the party faithful are interested in nominating only candidates who represent those respective views. But, when the primary season is over and the vote of party members is secured, the party nominee usually has no choice but to re-craft positions in an effort to appeal to the silent majority.

Members of the silent majority are neither liberal nor conservative. If they were liberal, they would be Democrats and if conservative, they would be Republicans. By definition, the silent majority is a blend of conservative and liberal ideals. The candidate with the best chance of winning is the candidate who is able to modify party positions to appeal to that blend. Most successful presidential candidates have followed this path, but not all. It's a tough balancing act to perform. Too much movement to the middle can offend the party faithful and cause them to sit out the election. On the other hand, if the candidate's shift in position is not convincing, the silent majority will consider it pandering, and turn away from the candidate who "doesn't seem to stand for anything." John Kerry's "flip-flopping" in this most recent campaign is a perfect example of the negative response this tactic can generate.

Reaching out to the middle can work well when an issue doesn't need to be defined in black or white terms, but instead has a range of possible solutions. This ambiguity allows the candidate to stake out a position that is closer to the middle of the continuum than true left or right. For example, a conservative position on tax cuts would be to cut everyone's taxes 10 percent, whether they were poor, middle class or wealthy. A liberal position would be to cut the taxes of the poor by 20 percent, the taxes of the middle class by 10 percent, and not to cut the taxes of the wealthy at all. A candidate from either party could move to the middle by proposing a 15 percent tax cut for the poor, a 10 percent cut for the middle class and a 5 percent cut for the wealthy. It's a compromise that still maintains a fair amount of integrity to each candidate's original position. This approach works on a wide variety of issues, not just those based on arithmetic. It has been successfully utilized on everything from health care to defense spending. In fact, this process of finding equilibrium between conservative and liberal ideals is quite healthy from the standpoint of stability. In a sense, the silent majority act as the gravitational force of politics, keeping the pendulum of either party from swinging wildly to the right or left. It wasn't necessarily designed that way. But, having a silent majority between the two parties has provided a very effective form of practical checks and balances in our political system, ensuring that our government moves with deliberation and patience instead of whipping from one extreme to the other.

This process of reaching out to the middle does not work well on binary issues. If there are only two possible solutions, black or white, where is the middle ground? Unfortunately, the cultural issues that are the focus of this discussion are essentially binary issues. For example, it's difficult to have a middle position on abortion. For the most part we are either for it or against it. Of course there are some who stake out a middle position by supporting only early-term abortion and opposing late-term abortion. Others believe middle ground can be found in opposing abortion except in the case of rape and incest. But these middle ground positions are usually not supported by any logical philosophy and therefore have no backbone of principle to hold them together. They are constructed to compromise only for the sake of compromise. Moral issues, such as abortion need to be based on and supported by moral principles. That fact makes all moral issues resistant to compromise. In the case of abortion, advocates believe the fetus is not an individual human life, and opponents believe it is. Where is the middle ground? It doesn't exist. Or consider gay marriage. On the right is the belief that marriage is a traditional institution and consists of the union of one man and one woman. On the left is the belief that a new form of marriage should be created that permits the union of one man with another man, or one woman with another woman. What is the possible middle ground? It certainly isn't to allow some same-sex marriages and not others. You are either for gay marriage or against it. With all moral issues, trying to find middle ground violates the fundamental principles on which the difference arises in the first place.

Though there is little or no room for compromise on moral issues when they are viewed independently, collections of issues can produce a variety of possible positions, some of which may have significantly higher levels of support than the current positions of the Democrats and Republicans. For example, the current positions of the two parties on the issues of the Culture War are:

Cultural Issue	Democrat	Republican
Abortion	Yes	No
Gun Control	Yes	No
School Prayer	No	Yes
Gay Marriage	Yes	No

Though it isn't likely to happen, what if the Democrats changed the configuration by switching from "yes" to "no" on abortion? Or, what if the Republicans switched from "no" to "yes" on gun control? Would these changes of position make either party more attractive to the voters in the middle? Regardless of the answer to these specific scenarios, the point is that increasing the number of options has the potential of attracting voters in the middle who do not support the current configuration of positions offered by the two major political parties.

I believe that the silent majority does not support either party's current configuration of positions on these moral issues. As long as the two parties maintain these positions, the Culture War will continue. There just isn't a significant majority in the middle that fully supports one view or the other. When it comes time to vote, a small majority can be won over by one side or the other. This election a small majority sided with the Republicans. Maybe next time the Democrats will prevail. Many who vote for the candidate of either party do so grudgingly and with a sense of despair. Grudgingly because we are compelled to select one candidate or the other even if we disagree with both, and with despair because we don't have an alternative that represents how we really feel on this collection of issues. How many times have you found yourself in a voting booth, selecting a candidate who you consider the "lesser of two evils"? I believe there is a lot of that going on relative to voting on these moral issues.

Is there a configuration of choices on the issues of the Culture War that would appeal to enough voters in the middle that a solid majority could be reached? I believe the following configuration would achieve that goal:

Cultural Issue	Democrat	Republican	An Alternative
Abortion	Yes	No	No
Gun Control	Yes	No	Yes
School Prayer	No	Yes	No
Gay Marriage	Yes	No	No

Why am I bold enough to predict this alternative platform would win the support of a majority of Americans? Because I believe that a significant majority of Americans still share the same fundamental values and those values applied to each of these issues independently leads to this collective conclusion. So, if traditional American values lead to this conclusion, why hasn't one or both of the political parties adopted this platform? Wouldn't it be in their best interest to take positions that appeal to a majority and are supported by their consistency with traditional American values? The answer is that I'm certain both parties believe that I'm wrong and that they have already based their current positions on the same fundamental American values I am referring to. I don't doubt that both parties are sincere in their adherence to core American values. Then how is it possible that three different conclusions—Republican, Democrat and this alternative—could be reached from the same set of core values? The answer is found in the natural conflict that exists between two primary American values: respecting individual freedom and ensuring the common good.

There is often a natural tension between these two principles. It's usually resolved by the answer to the following question: Does the action of an individual in any way interfere with the individual rights of another, or cause significant harm to society in general? If the answer is "no," we are inclined by our principles to allow the individual the right to do it, even though it might be something we personally disagree with. If the answer is "yes,"—meaning we believe it will infringe on another's rights, or perhaps is detrimental to society in general—we forbid the action. We generally find the decision to restrict individual freedom easy to make when the action of one individual clearly infringes on the rights of another individual. For example, we do not allow any individual the freedom to kill his neighbor, no matter how great that desire might be. Nor do we allow a person to take the property of another, no matter how much the person might desire the property as his or her own.

We find it far more difficult to restrict individual freedom when an action does not have an obvious, immediate and direct effect on another individual, but does have potential negative effects on society in general. This favoritism of individual rights at the expense of the common good is evident in the number of societal risks we are willing to accept in an effort to preserve individual freedom. As an example, laws in all states allow adults to purchase and consume alcoholic beverages, even though we know it's inevitable that some heavy drinkers will drive while drunk. We know accidents will happen, and innocent citizens will lose their lives. The decision to allow drinking is based on the calculus that the vast majority of drinkers are harming no one but themselves and that harm to another is rare enough that we can tolerate it. In addition, to further mitigate the risk, as a form of deterrence, we impose severe penalties on any who are caught driving while drunk.

One of the primary reasons we are reluctant to curb individual freedoms that might be detrimental to society is that determining how, or to what extent these freedoms are "detrimental" can be a very subjective process. It's not easy to project the cumulative effects of individual acts on an entire society, especially when the effects are felt over a long period of time. The subjective nature of many of these decisions is made obvious in the inconsistency of many of the laws we have enacted that restrict individual behavior. For example, consider the laws that regulate the use of marijuana. Marijuana is outlawed in every state, and stiff penalties are imposed on any individual who uses or even possesses it. Marijuana and alcohol have essentially the same effect on an individual who uses either to excess. Why is marijuana completely banned and alcohol not? In this particular example, the decision not to ban alcohol is heavily influenced by the fact that alcohol consumption is widely ingrained in our culture. Alcoholic beverages have enjoyed a prominent place in American life since long before this country was even formally created. During a short period in our history, we actually experimented with the idea of banning alcohol consumption. But this prohibition was repealed after a short period of time because so many people were breaking the law that it couldn't be enforced. The public reached the conclusion that it was better to deal with the negative side effects of alcohol consumption than to deal with overwhelming criminal activity spawned by prohibition.

Marijuana, on the other hand, doesn't have the same history of widespread public acceptance and usage. Its constituency is small enough to manage. The difference in the treatment of the two substances is also partly commercial in nature. Significant, legitimate businesses have been built up around the manufacture, distribution and sale of alcoholic beverages. This industry creates jobs and profits that are used as leverage against any attempt to regulate it. Though there are substantial commercial gains made in the manufacture, distribution and sale of marijuana, the profits are not made in the legitimate business world. The relatively small size of the marijuana "industry" makes prohibiting the drug a manageable task. As this example illustrates, it can be a real struggle to find the proper balance between preserving individual freedom and protecting the common good. In spite of our natural inclination to err on the side of individual freedom, our duty to society often requires us to enact laws that restrict individual behavior.

You might wonder what this lengthy digression has to do with the Culture War. I think it's important to understand the tension between these two principles because I believe it's the root cause of the Culture War. Our tendency to favor individual freedom even when we personally disapprove of a particular action is evident in our reluctance to take a stand on the moral issues that divide us. By any measure imaginable, the number of people who actually participate in abortion, the number who would participate in gay marriage and the number who are adamant about owning guns or having prayer in schools is clearly a minority. Most of us have made the decision that we personally disagree on all counts. We would not practice abortion, don't support gay marriage, don't care to own guns and believe that prayer is to be practiced at church and in the home, not in a public school. Though we make those personal choices, we are extremely reluctant to inhibit others from practicing the opposite. At its best, this willingness to allow others the freedom to act in ways we might

personally disagree with is a noble sentiment. But it isn't noble sentiment alone that keeps us from restricting minority behavior that can
be extremely disruptive and harmful to society in general. All too
often it is nothing more than an easy copout for a reluctant majority
who are unwilling to take tough stands on difficult issues. A significant number of Americans, especially those who belong to the silent
majority, have a moral position on these issues but have been unwilling to take a stand. This unwillingness to take a stand has been detrimental to our society and will become increasingly so as the
cumulative effects of these practices add up over the coming years.

The chapters that follow make the case that the majority of Americans are against abortion and gay marriage but are in favor of gun
control and the separation of church and state. The following chapters also assert that the majority should take a tough stand on these
moral issues even though it means restricting the behavior of a sizeable and vocal minority. Currently the two sides in this battle are
nearly equal in strength—Republicans on one side, Democrats on the
other. The silent majority, in essence, is sitting it out. We are locked
in a stalemate in this political "tug of war" and the detrimental consequences in the near term are obvious to everyone. The divisiveness of
the Culture War has inflamed partisanship to levels we have seldom,
if ever, experienced before. This partisanship has rendered our government dysfunctional on many fronts and has divided the country
into red and blue territories where the inhabitants sometimes wonder
when and how the United States became the "divided states." As bad
as the short term consequences are, they pale in comparison to the
potential long term damage they could cause. Our form of government works very well when compromise on policy is possible. In the
absence of common values, compromise will be increasingly difficult
to construct, and our government will be increasingly and perpetually
partisan and dysfunctional. But the real tragedy will be the irreversible
erosion of the moral foundation of America. Abortion, firearm violence, gay marriage and the preferential treatment of religion represent values that are significantly at odds with the values that form the

foundation of our government and represent the real genius of America. The erosion and loss of this unique moral foundation would be a tragedy not only for current and future generations of Americans, but for the entire world. There is much at stake in this Culture War.

The silent majority has the ability to get off the sidelines, join the battle, and end this "tug of war." It's a game with serious long term consequences, and citizens who have been silent for far too long have an obligation to speak up now. There will always be a sizeable opposing minority no matter which positions are taken on these four issues. Thus, the Culture War cannot be won in the same sense that real wars are won—there will never be a complete end to hostilities. But a position that is more consistent with the values of the silent majority can shift the balance of power considerably, containing the Culture War and reducing it to a nuisance instead of the divisive and detrimental force it is today.

Abortion

If we envisioned the Culture War as a wall that separates red and blue America, abortion would undoubtedly be the foundation of that wall. If such strongly held differences of opinion concerning abortion did not exist, the three remaining cultural issues would not have caused the divisiveness that now characterizes the Culture War. I'm not trying to minimize the moral importance of the other issues. It's true that on their own merits each of these issues would be a significant source of conflict. But when it comes to the Culture War, it's clear that abortion is the primary battlefield.

Why does this issue continue to generate such passionate opposition more than 30 years after the landmark Supreme Court decision—Roe v. Wade—that declared abortion legal? I think one of the primary reasons is that the legality of abortion was determined by judges and not by ballots. It's not my aim to enter into a legal discussion of the pros and cons of the Supreme Court decision. In fact, I'm willing to concede that the decision made perfect legal sense to the Supreme Court of 1973 or any Supreme Court that might follow it. But the High Court's decision was unfortunate because it was the exact opposite of how the majority of Americans felt about abortion at the time. In fact, prior to this ruling, nearly every state had enacted laws that banned abortion. Even the few states that didn't totally ban abortion, strictly limited its practice. It's important in any discussion of abortion to remember that when citizens and legislators were allowed to vote "yes" or "no" on abortion, the choice was almost universally "no" everywhere in the United States. America had decided by a significant majority, that abortion was a personal freedom that society should not tolerate. The Supreme Court decision negated every restriction of abortion that was in place at the time, not because the laws were right or wrong in a moral sense, but because the Court decided that the Constitution of the United States did not inherently provide a "legal" way for states to ban abortion. Such a ruling says nothing about whether it's good or bad for a society to allow abortion. It just means that our Constitution, written over 225 years ago, and amended very infrequently since, has no language within it that currently provides legal justification for any state law that bans abortion.

Our courts function in a legal realm, not a moral realm. This is an important distinction to understand, especially with regard to moral issues. It's surprising to me how many Americans view Supreme Court decisions as if they were handed down on stone tablets from on High. I realize there are many who don't feel that way on a variety of specific Court decisions. But I honestly believe that too many Americans think that a decision from the Supreme Court is always legally accurate and is always in the best interests of America. Unfortunately, all Court decisions require human judgment and legal accuracy is not always the outcome. And even if legal accuracy is achieved, it has nothing to do with the morality of the decision.

How is it possible that legally accurate court decisions could be damaging to the country? The Supreme Court settles legal disputes by determining which side in an argument is most consistent with the principles found in the Constitution of the United States. I, along with nearly everyone else in this country, agree that the Constitution is the most remarkable foundation for government ever invented by man. It certainly is an inspired document, perhaps by God if you are so inclined to believe, and certainly by the genius of a brilliant generation of leaders who founded this nation. But in spite of the reverence it inspires and deserves it's not inconsistent to also acknowledge that our Constitution isn't perfect. In its original form, it didn't even include the Bill of Rights. It would be difficult for us to imagine the

Constitution without the Bill of Rights. Without these first ten amendments to the original document the Constitution would be a far less impressive source of individual rights. In fact, the first ten amendments are probably, more often than not, the rights we associate with the Constitution itself—freedom of speech, freedom of the press, the right to bear arms and so on. And what does the original Constitution say about voting rights for women? It was silent on the issue, leaving it up to each individual state. The 14th amendment was a relatively recent addition, passed in 1920, that granted all women the right to vote.

It isn't surprising that a written constitution would fail to include every necessary and desirable article in its first form. We shouldn't even be too surprised if some articles included in the document are in retrospect flat out wrong. I think almost everyone would agree that the greatest shortcoming of the original Constitution was its treatment of slaves. When you consider the great respect for individual freedom and human rights expressed in the document, it would have seemed that an outright ban of slavery naturally would have been included. But in one of the greatest inconsistencies imaginable, slaves were given just the opposite treatment. In the Constitution, slaves were not recognized as individuals with rights, they were considered the property of white citizens. To add insult to injury, five slaves counted as only three constituents for purposes of apportioning House seats. Imagine the effect of this provision. Slaves themselves could not vote, but as the number of slaves in a state increased, so did the voting power of the state through increased representation in the House of Representatives. In essence, the Constitution withheld all human rights from slaves, declared that one slave counted as only three-fifths of a person and encouraged the growth of slavery through the incentive of apportioning additional House seats as slavery increased. It took nearly a century and the great tragedy of civil war to correct this egregious flaw in the Constitution.

We should respect and honor the Constitution, but it's a fact that much of what we respect and honor about it today was not included in its original form. And it's very clear that the writers of the document realized it would not be perfect. They wisely included an amendment process to correct it. The Constitution started out as an exceptional document, but has been improved significantly through the amendment process. Rather than assume it is perfect, as we often do, we should assume that we will find additional flaws or shortcomings in the Constitution that need correcting through the amendment process.

Likewise, we should respect decisions rendered by the Supreme Court, but we should not be under the illusion that every decision made by the Court is morally sound, or for that matter, even legally correct. The Court is an assemblage of nine legal experts who have the difficult task of determining the constitutionality of issues that are by definition complex and difficult to reconcile with the Constitution. If the issues were not complex and difficult they would be resolved in lower courts and never be elevated to the Supreme Court for a final decision. It should not be surprising that more often than not the Court is divided in its opinions. Unanimity is a rarity. Many of the most important decisions of the Court have been decided by 5 justices in favor of the majority opinion and 4 justices disagreeing with the decision. Does that mean that the 4 dissenting justices were legally incorrect, less intellectually capable or morally inferior to their 5 colleagues? Of course not. What it really indicates is that men and women of great legal skill, considerable intellect and a sincere desire to do what is right can reach different conclusions when considering complex legal issues. And therefore, decisions of the Supreme Court are far from infallible. In fact, they are often decided by a slim majority within the Court and who knows what the verdict might be if considered by the legal community at large or a reconstituted Court at a different point in time.

In spite of the debatable nature of many Supreme Court decisions, many Americans insist on casting decisions that are in harmony with their own personal beliefs as inviolate and not subject to debate or further consideration. The recent Senate confirmation hearings for the appointment of John Roberts as Chief Justice provided many examples of this self-serving rationalization. The clearest example was provided by the Chairman of the Senate Judiciary Committee considering the appointment, Arlen Specter, a Republican Senator from Pennsylvania. Specter has made it very clear over the course of his Senate career that he believes very strongly that abortion is a right that is both morally desirable and legally correct. In his questioning of candidate Roberts, Specter sought to ensure that his personal views on abortion would be continued in perpetuity through two means: 1) convincing Roberts—and indirectly any American who was tuning in to the hearings—that Roe v. Wade was "settled law" and could not by overturned, and 2) subtly threatening to vote against Roberts if he did not agree. Specter's staff had prepared a very large chart that indicated all of the instances in the past 33 years when the Supreme Court had the opportunity to overrule Roe v. Wade and chose not to do it. The chart was prominently displayed in the hearing room as Specter tutored Roberts and the nation on the principle of "stare decisis," or legal precedent. The phrase is obviously of Latin origin and its English translation is "to stand by things decided." It's a phrase that has been co-opted by the legal community for the very purpose of making the principle of legal precedent sound eternal and unchangeable, as if having roots in ancient Rome would sufficiently immunize it from challenge. This legal practice of using foreign language instead of plain English to keep the average American from understanding what is going on would be laughable if it were not so effective. But in this case, Specter decided to resort to very plain English after establishing the principle in Latin terms by asking Roberts, "Would you think that Roe might be a super-duper precedent?" That's right. In his blind desire to ensure that Roe would not be overturned a well-trained lawyer and distinguished Senator invented a new legal term on national TV. Roe has now entered the pantheon of super-duper precedents.

Senator Specter graciously handled the humor that his remarks generated. But the principle he espoused—that once the Supreme

Court decides something it is never open to debate again—is not a laughing matter. If he truly believed that about all constitutional precedents, imagine what Specter would have been arguing in the Senate of 1860. Imagine the size of the chart he could have constructed to show the "stare decisis" foundation for the practice of slavery. After all, it had been the recognized law of the land for more than 70 years at that time. Or imagine Chairman Specter's chart to deny women the right to vote in 1920. With more than 130 years of precedent denying women the right to vote his staff would have been burning the midnight oil to construct a massive chart for his civics lesson to the nation. Would a time traveling Senator Specter have done such a thing? Absolutely not. His track record on these two issues is clear. He would have been leading the charge to bring down the legal precedents that allowed slavery and treated women as silent partners in democracy. His arguments in the Roberts hearings were not intellectually honest. They were the all-too-human rationalization of a man blinded by his desire to preserve something he believes in very strongly. Unfortunately, he has many colleagues in the Senate who are equally intent on creating a court that reflects their own personal beliefs. Through this legal form of Darwinism many capable, honest and worthy jurists will never be considered or, if appointed, tossed aside as only the like-minded survive to sit on the Supreme Court. And it's obviously a process that goes both ways. Many are diligently working for the opposite result on the abortion issue. It hasn't always been that way, but the moral issues of the Culture War invariably lead to deciding between fundamental American values, with all roads of resolution converging on the Supreme Court. What was once the least political of the three branches of government is now in danger of becoming a political body whose members serve lifetime appointments and are not subject to any democratic form of accountability. On top of that, the political philosophy of any new jurist is determined by the prevailing political party at the time of appointment to the Court. That means the political leanings of the Court are essentially determined by chance. This trend should give us even more reason to accept the fact that Supreme Court decisions are not always perfect.

It's because of the imperfect nature of the Constitution and of the justices who interpret it, that Supreme Court decisions can be legally inaccurate, and even if legally accurate, they can be morally dead wrong. Fortunately, almost always, Court decisions are both legally correct and from the perspective of an overwhelming majority, morally sound. But there are occasional exceptions—Roe v. Wade is one of those exceptions.

You might be surprised by the assertion that abortion doesn't have the support of a majority of Americans. You've likely heard exactly the opposite expressed repeatedly and authoritatively by abortion advocates and sympathetic journalists. But constant repetition of false information doesn't make it true. A false impression is created by those who massage polling data to achieve results that indicate a very slim majority supporting abortion. The following recent poll illustrates the point:

Abortion Should Be:	Legal In All Cases	Legal In Most Cases	Illegal In Most Cases	Illegal In All Cases	Unsure
	21%	34%	25%	17%	3%

—ABC News/Washington Post Poll, December 16–19, 2004

How do you think this poll was reported in the media? Of course the headline was that a majority of Americans are in favor of legal abortion. But this is a convenient and incomplete assessment of the polling data. We should first recognize that 55 percent is hardly a substantial majority. When the potential margin of error is factored in, the actual support might be closer to 50 percent, the slimmest of majorities. But more importantly, we should recognize that this particular interpretation of the poll very conveniently glosses over the fact that only 21 percent of people surveyed favor abortion in all cases, which is in essence what Roe v. Wade has become in practice.

Thus, only around one-fifth of the nation supports the Court's decision. Furthermore, the question "Do you think abortion should be legal in most cases?" is ambiguous enough that survey respondents could interpret it to mean anything from "abortion should be legal in almost all cases" to "abortion should be legal only under a small number of specific circumstances." When a more discerning set of questions was asked in another recent poll, the following results were recorded:

Abortion Should Be:	Legal In All Cases	Legal In Most Cases	**Illegal With A Few Exceptions***	Illegal In All Cases	Unsure
	24%	19%	41%	12%	4%

*Exceptions: cases of rape, incest and to save the mother's life

—Los Angeles Times Poll, January 15–17, 2005

Isn't the difference interesting and enlightening? Again we find slightly more than one-fifth in complete support of Roe v. Wade, but notice the significant decrease in support for the "most of the time" category when rape, incest and saving the life of the mother are identified as specific exceptions. With that significant clarification, we find that 53 percent of respondents believe that abortion should either be illegal without exception, or available only in case of rape, incest or to protect the life of the mother. So the headline from this more discerning poll is that only 24 percent of Americans support unrestricted abortion—what Roe v. Wade has become in practice—and an overwhelming majority of 72 percent oppose it. In addition, a small majority are even in favor of banning abortion entirely except in the case of rape, incest or to protect the life of the mother. Of course that headline was never written.

I readily acknowledge that 53 percent against abortion is not a substantial majority and that other polls can and will show slightly different results. But at the end of the day, I think everyone can agree that unrestricted or even slightly restricted abortion is not supported by a significant majority. It is either a dead-even proposition or weighted slightly in one direction or the other. Neither side can claim a majority position. The nearly equal division between the two sides helps to explain why the disagreement is so fierce and has carried on for so long.

Though Americans are equally divided on whether or not abortion ought to be available, when asked directly if they think having an abortion is wrong, an entirely different picture emerges:

"Regardless of whether you think abortion should be allowed or not, do you personally believe having an abortion is wrong?"

	Yes, think it is wrong	No	Not Sure
All	59%	34%	7%
Women	62%	32%	6%

—CNN/Time Poll, January 15–16, 2003

Any way you look at this data, it's clear that a solid majority believes abortion is wrong. It's a 60 percent majority in raw numbers and, proportionately, those who think abortion is wrong outnumber those who think it is okay nearly two to one.

These polls are not anomalies. When questions about abortion are asked in this manner, the polls are amazingly consistent. We could argue a few percentage points one way or the other, but the bottom line is still the same. A solid majority believes that abortion is wrong, and yet roughly 50 percent of us would not restrict others from having one. It might seem that mathematically, it just doesn't add up—that roughly 10 percent of us are having it both ways. But this is not the calculus of a single question. It's the combination of two separate but related questions. Simply put, a majority of Americans believe that abortion is wrong, but not everyone in that majority is willing to impose that belief on others. It's a perfect example of the conflict I discussed in the previous chapter. How do we determine the appropriate balance between respecting individual freedom, and ensuring the common good? Abortion is not an issue that is easy to deal with in this regard. It's always easier to come down on the side of the common good if the individual action obviously interferes with the rights of another. Unfortunately, the "other" in the case of abortion is not readily visible. Out of sight, out of mind is not a minor factor in this decision making process. There is also the complicating reality that many believe a fetus is not necessarily a human life and are willing to leave that determination to the mother and her doctor. For these reasons, approximately half of us have reached the conclusion that abortion is a personal action that doesn't harm anyone but the mother. However, there is still one final test we should apply to strike the appropriate balance between these two conflicting principles: Though abortion might not appear to have immediate, undesirable effects on another individual, does it have potential negative effects on society in general? Again, for at least half of us, the answer is no. Thus, on abortion, we have reached roughly a fifty-fifty balance of those favoring individual freedom and those favoring the common good.

There are two additional arguments that should be factored into the individual rights side of this equation. First, many who personally think abortion is wrong are simply unwilling to take a strong stand on the issue. In fact, they just wish it would go away. Their attitude is, "as long as it's not hurting me, even though I personally would not do it, why get involved?" The second factor is the astounding lack of public dialogue on abortion. Your initial reaction to that statement might be disbelief. However, don't confuse loud, emotional and frequent monologue with rational public dialogue. I don't remember exactly when the battle over abortion settled into the "pro-choice" and "pro-life" monologues, but it must have been shortly after Roe v. Wade was decided. It's a well established fact that people have a hard time talking and listening at the same time. For 30 years there has been a lot of talk about abortion and precious little listening. I guess it's not surprising though, considering the passion of the advocates who are deeply committed to one side or the other. That's natural. What is surprising is the lack of participation by those who are either in the middle or only leaning one way or the other. As discussed previously, the silent majority earned its nickname for good reason. In a two party system, a third voice has a hard time being heard. But in this case, there is more to it than that. Most of us feel uncomfortable and inadequate in expressing our personal opinion on abortion, because our opinion is influenced significantly by our religious faith. It's not easy to explain a position that is primarily based on feeling and faith, and not entirely on logic. Dialogue with religious overtones is difficult to express, so it is avoided. We've all likely heard the admonition that to preserve harmony in a relationship we should avoid discussion of politics and religion. Abortion is a topic that is radioactive on both counts.

In an attempt to overcome this shortage of real public dialogue on the topic of abortion, the next few chapters present my own perspective on the primary points of conflict in the debate. It should be clear to the reader at this point that I believe abortion shouldn't be allowed. I believe we have made a mistake in not fully considering the harm abortion causes to individuals and society in general. It's my hope the chapters that follow will effectively communicate why I believe we ought to tip the balance in favor of the common good on this issue.

When Does Life Begin

The moment at which a human fetus becomes an individual human life is, of course, central to any discussion of abortion. No rational American would support abortion if he or she felt an individual human life was at stake. Those who support abortion on demand must certainly believe that a fetus does not become a human life until birth occurs. And those who are against abortion at anytime for any reason must certainly believe that the fetus is a human being from the moment of conception. But a significant number of Americans are caught somewhere between these two extremes. This large segment of the electorate, mostly comprised of the silent majority, doesn't believe life begins as early as conception, but does believe it begins at a point long before birth. Some in this group believe life begins soon after conception and are generally against abortion at any time. Others believe life begins a considerable time after conception and generally support abortion in the early months of pregnancy. Some in this latter group are willing to support abortion up to three months, others up to six. Although many different opinions exist concerning when abortion should be allowed, the determining factor that should inform every American's position on the subject is the answer to the question: "When does life begin?" Therefore any serious dialogue concerning abortion must begin with this question.

It's such an obvious fact that the entire abortion debate hinges on this one question that you would expect it to be a topic of considerable public discussion. Quite the opposite is true. In your experience, do you recall any serious in-depth public debate over when life begins? Have you ever heard an abortion advocate explain why he or she thinks a fetus is not an individual human life? I doubt it. I know I haven't. Why do those who believe that life doesn't begin until birth avoid talking about it? They dodge this critical question because their position is illogical and indefensible. Instead of engaging in a discussion of this central question the proponents of abortion have been very successful at changing the subject. They insist that abortion has nothing to do with whether or not a fetus is a human life. It's all about a mother's right to choose. They even label themselves as pro-choice to avoid having to explain why they are pro-abortion. Pro-abortion groups have had astounding success playing this shell game that draws attention away from the real issue and convinces many people that abortion is all about a woman's right to choose. True to our American heritage, most of us are automatically sympathetic to arguments that favor the protection of individual rights; so, many are following the shell containing the right to choose and have lost track of the other shell. Too many have forgotten that under the other shell the central question remains. A question that, if answered, might lead to the conclusion that a mother's right to choose infringes on another individual's right to live.

Unfortunately, on the other side of the ledger, the pro-lifers are willing to talk about when life begins, but haven't been at all convincing even though the argument for life is much easier to make than the argument against life. But if that's so, why has the pro-life movement failed so miserably to make the case? It's because, in most instances, the argument has been made on the basis of religious faith. These faith-based arguments are certainly convincing to those already of the same faith, but perhaps not to those of other faiths and certainly not to those of who don't subscribe to any faith. It's true that a Christian argument appeals to a large number of Americans, but the Christian faith is not monolithic. Not all Christian denominations share the same belief about when life actually begins. In fact, there are many self-proclaimed progressive denominations that support abortion. However, the real impediment to achieving a majority position based on Christian faith is not doctrinal difference. The vast majority of Christian denominations believe that life begins at conception. The problem is that large numbers of Christians are not active in their faith, or they may be active but disagree with this particular article of faith. Though nearly 85 percent of Americans are Christian, only half of that number attends church on a regular basis. Many don't even know the articles of faith of the church they claim membership in. If every Christian believed and practiced the articles of faith of their own denomination, we would long ago have found a way to stop the practice of abortion. So, even though Christians are an overwhelming majority, the Christian faith-based argument that life begins at conception has been ineffective essentially because it has fallen on deaf ears.

Besides not convincing even the faithful, the faith-based argument has provided pro-abortion groups with another shell to use in the shell game. Whenever a faith-based argument is used against abortion a charge of religious intolerance is sure to follow. The contents of this shell position the pro-abortion groups as defenders of another of the most cherished of American values—freedom of religion. Now pro-abortion groups can claim they are not only standing up for a woman's right to choose, they are also protecting her from religious intolerance. You couldn't find two more appealing labels than pro-choice and pro-religious-tolerance. Whoever created the public relations campaign for abortion deserves recognition for developing one of the most impressive schemes ever devised. By keeping everyone's attention focused on the attractive but peripheral issues of individual choice and religious tolerance, pro-abortion advocates avoid the central issue of when life begins. I suppose it was inevitable that attention would need to be deflected from the central issue. Constructing a convincing argument that a fetus is not a living being the entire nine months it is in the womb would be impossible.

If pro-abortionists don't want to talk about when human life begins and faith based pro-life arguments have been ineffective, where do we turn to answer the question? We are left with three possible sources: law, science and our own common sense. It may come as a surprise to you that current law makes it very clear when human life begins. I know I found it very surprising. I always thought that when the Supreme Court decided Roe v. Wade, the justices only concluded that abortion was not specifically banned by the Constitution. But their decision went far beyond a simple "yes" or "no" on abortion by defining when abortion would be allowed. Specifically, the Court ruled that during the first and second trimesters of pregnancy states cannot bar any woman from obtaining an abortion from a licensed physician. In the third trimester states may regulate abortion to protect fetal life, but not at the expense of the woman's life or health. I found this truly incredible. As I mentioned in the previous chapter, I don't doubt the Supreme Court's finding that there is nothing in the Constitution that would specifically restrict the practice of abortion. I have absolutely no problem with the Court's legal reasoning in that regard. But to take the additional step of defining when abortion is or is not allowed during pregnancy cannot be construed as a legal interpretation by any stretch of the imagination. I am 100 percent certain there is nothing in the Constitution that specifies that pregnancy should be divided into trimesters and further stipulates in which of them abortion is to be allowed. But that is exactly what the Court decided.

Even more astounding than the fact that the justices constructed the trimester test from whole cloth is that it also implicitly establishes when life begins. According to the Court, life begins the moment a fetus enters the third trimester. When you look at the system the Court created, you can reach no other conclusion. The only possible reason to protect the fetus in the third trimester is that the Court felt at this point the fetus was an individual life and therefore was entitled to the same protections that the Constitution grants to all Americans. How in the world did the Supreme Court decide that a fetus in the first two trimesters was not yet a human life but suddenly crosses the threshold of life at the beginning of the third trimester? Of course it had to do with the real life experiences of the justices, who were certainly aware of the fact that many premature babies, born during the third trimester, were known to have lived and developed normally in spite of the early delivery. Conversely, at that time, premature births in the first or second trimester were always unsuccessful.

Thus Roe v. Wade did much more than just strike down laws restricting abortion. The decision also implicitly specified when life begins. And the Court's implicit decision conveniently allows us to pinpoint when life begins with mathematical accuracy. A typical pregnancy lasts approximately 40 weeks. The first trimester begins with conception and ends with week 13. The second trimester spans weeks 14 through 26. The third begins with week 27 and culminates in the delivery of the baby. By law then, life begins at the start of the 27th week of pregnancy. It might not be explicitly stated that way, but there is no other logical conclusion that can be reached. By allowing abortion through week 26 but prohibiting it from then on, the Court has implicitly determined that life begins at 27 weeks.

I've never had a reason to study the specifics of Roe v. Wade until I determined to write this book. I suspect my prior level of understanding of this monumental court case is consistent with the understanding of most Americans. Most of us really don't have any reason to go beyond a superficial understanding of Roe v. Wade. It's enough to know that this decision legalized abortion. I can't possibly find the words to explain how surprised and shocked I am at my own lack of knowledge about the full extent of the Court's decision, especially its specificity concerning the timing of the origin of life in the womb. Admittedly, I am not an expert in Constitutional law, but it doesn't take much more than a little common sense to realize that there is nothing in the Constitution that would allow the Court to determine during which trimesters a fetus should be protected and during which it should not. It would seem to me that the Constitution would require the justices either to allow all abortion or none at all. But instead the justices got caught in a legal and moral dilemma. They concluded that the Constitution provided them no legal cover to restrict abortion, but their personal experience and moral values led them to conclude they could not allow viable babies in the third trimester to be aborted. Though the Court attempted to side-step the issue of viability—the likelihood the fetus would develop into an individual life outside the womb—in actuality it is clear in the Roe v. Wade decision that viability was not only a factor, it was clearly the most significant factor. So the Court entered into the realm of crafting a decision based on both law and personal wisdom. They in essence "played Solomon" and decided the development of the fetus in the womb would be divided into legally unprotected pre-life for the first six months and legally protected, not to be aborted, separate and individual life, in the last three months.

If you are not familiar with the life of King Solomon, he is most often remembered for his encounter with two women who both claimed to be the mother of the same child. Solomon was asked to judge between the two of them, but found it impossible with the existing evidence to declare one or the other the birth mother. At that point, he suggested that he would resolve the dispute by splitting the baby in half, giving each claimant one half of the child. Solomon's decision caused the real birth mother to proclaim she would give the baby to the other woman rather than allow Solomon to kill the baby. Solomon wisely recognized that the true mother would react in such a way. He kept the baby whole and alive, awarding possession to the real mother who had spoken up in defense of her child. For this insight into human behavior King Solomon has been recognized for centuries as a preeminent example of a man using uncommon wisdom in a manner worthy of emulation.

In the case of Roe v. Wade, the Court, in a very real sense has "split the baby." A fetus less than 27 weeks in the womb is not a baby, but the instant it reaches 27 weeks, it is. The justices who decided in favor of Roe v. Wade were likely quite proud of the human wisdom they applied in the decision. But unlike Solomon's decision which was validated once and forever by the immediate response of the birth mother, validation of the supposed wisdom of Roe v. Wade is dependent on the application of science to instances of premature birth.

And though science was initially kind to the justices, as often happens when clever human minds craft what appear to be intelligent solutions to complex problems, the passage of time has not been kind to the trimester system. Advances in medical care since the time of Roe v. Wade have made the third trimester definition extremely problematic. Survivability of premature birth has improved considerably since then. Consider the following recent table concerning the survival rate for premature births:

Weeks	21 or less	22	23	24	25	26	27
Survival Rate	0%	0–10%	10–35%	40–70%	50–80%	80–90%	90%+

—Premature Infants, Encyclopedia of Nursing and Allied Health, by R.N. Nadine M. Jacobson

Remember, the court ruling established the beginning of week 27 as the time at which the fetus in the womb becomes a protected baby. From these statistics, and many others that substantially agree with them, it should be clear that any fetus aborted after week 21 has some chance of viability, increasing to near surety by week 27. Unfortunately for the Court, medical science has improved to the point that the Court's selection of the 27th week as the cutoff point is now five weeks beyond the point at which babies can be born and survive. Recently retired Supreme Court Justice Sandra Day O'Conner recognized and described this problem when she wrote in a well-known dissenting opinion in 1982, "The Roe framework is clearly on a collision course with itself." It would be difficult to improve upon her characterization of the flawed nature of the trimester system. It was clear to her back in 1982 that science and technology were gradually pushing viability earlier into the second trimester and perhaps someday would even reach into the first trimester. She was obviously right, but I suspect even she has been surprised that only 23 years later the Roe framework is now fully five weeks out of whack. A five week error in a forty week process—a miscalculation of more than 12 percent—might be acceptable in some processes but is a profoundly tragic miscalculation in a matter of life and death. And the magnitude of this tragic error will only grow with time.

Justice O'Conner's dissenting comments in 1982 gave great hope to pro-life forces that she would eventually have the opportunity to participate in overturning the flawed Roe framework. But for reasons known only to her, when presented with the opportunity in 1992 to strike a significant blow to Roe v. Wade, she sided with the majority and reaffirmed the original decision. She expressed the opinion that a Pennsylvania law that required a wife to notify her husband before proceeding with an abortion placed an "undue burden" on the wife's right to choose and the Pennsylvania statute was struck down. It was a disappointing decision to many and one that is hard to fathom in light of her earlier recognition of the flawed nature of Roe v. Wade. Instead of doing something to minimize the impact of a decision that was now not only on a collision course with itself, but was actually in the midst of that very collision, she could find no reason to change course and prevent further damage. It's ironic that this same Pennsylvania case is now at the center of the upcoming Senate hearing for the most recent appointee to the Supreme Court, Judge Samuel Alito, who, even more ironically, is nominated to replace the retiring O'Conner. He was the lone vote in the 3rd U.S. Circuit Court of Appeals to support the law that Justice O'Conner famously, or infamously depending on which side you line up with, helped to shoot down. If he manages to survive the Senate process and takes his place on the Court, will his obvious concerns with the legality of Roe v. Wade compel him to vote to overturn it or at least modify the faulty framework? As we have learned with Justices O'Conner, Souter, Kennedy and many of their colleagues over the past 30 years, in spite of the obvious flaws in the trimester system, members of the Court are reluctant to overturn the original ruling. Is it out of respect for settled law? Is it out of respect for the reputations of their predecessors on the Court? Is it because they believe abortion ought to be legal even though the current legal foundation that allows the practice of abortion is seriously flawed? Who knows? But we do know that an intellectual system that has no legal basis in the Constitution was put in place to protect viable human life in the final trimester of pregnancy and it is now fatally flawed. This failed attempt by the Court to emulate Solomon demonstrates quite clearly why the Supreme Court ought to stick to matters of legal interpretation and steer clear of the intersection of science and morality. The Court now finds itself with a legal framework that is no longer valid and yet finds itself more committed to "stare decisis"—respecting the legal precedent established by Roe v. Wade—than to correcting the flawed decision. To twist a well known phrase a bit to fit the situation in which the Court now finds itself: "Oh what tangled webs we weave..."

Surprisingly, science has been more circumspect than the courts in defining when life begins. Of course, you can find scientists who are willing to express an opinion, and those opinions vary from one end of the trimester system to the other. Some say life begins at conception. Some say it doesn't begin until natural birth. And others mark the origin of life at any of a wide variety of points between those two extremes. But for the most part, scientists have been wise enough to avoid the obvious ethical and moral dilemma that is sure to follow any specific declaration of when life begins. Too bad the Supreme Court of 1973 lacked the same humility and common sense. Unlike the Supreme Court, seasoned scientists learn early on that the passage of time can make yesterday's scientific theory look like out-dated science fiction today. Like all fields of science, biology and other life sciences are continually evolving, frequently invalidating or updating previously held theories. A scientist who goes out on a limb with a prediction of when life begins is likely to regret it at a later date.

When posed in a scientific framework, the question of when life begins only introduces more questions and few concrete answers. When does life begin? The scientist first has to answer the question, "What is life?" If the scientist is able to find a satisfactory answer to that question, he next has to answer the question, "What is meant by begin?" Such parsing of the English language was humorous when done by President Clinton, but these questions are not trivial to the scientist and the scientific process. Can you imagine the wide range of answers to these two questions in a scientific sense? Does our definition of life begin at the cellular level? Individual cells are certainly a form of life. Or do we go to the other extreme and define life only as fully formed and functional human beings? And what exactly is the beginning? When the separate components capable of forming life come together? Or when the life form has reached its full capability? The answers run the full spectrum of possibilities—you can find some support for human life beginning at any point from conception to delivery. The net result is that science offers us no generally agreed upon definition of when human life begins.

Though science does not define when life begins, it certainly offers us much evidence that needs to be considered in making that determination. Recent advances in science provide insights into how the fetus is developing in the womb that were not imaginable even a few years ago. New technologies that monitor vital functions, and even provide electronic images from within the womb, now provide us with information that seriously questions the wisdom of the trimester abortion system. Consider the following characteristics and images of fetal development in the first two trimesters:

Month	Characteristics	Images
Two	• All essential organs have at least begun to form. • Arms and legs have lengthened with foot and hand areas distinguishable. • Hands and feet have digits, but may still be webbed. • Elbows and toes visible. • Facial features continue to develop.	

Three	• The head comprises nearly half of the fetus' size. • The face is well formed. • Tooth buds appear for the baby teeth. • Limbs are long and thin. • The fetus can make a fist with its fingers. • Genitals appear well differentiated. • Red blood cells are produced in the liver.	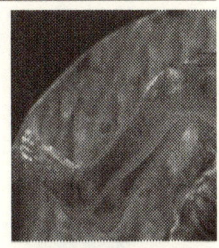
Four	• A fine hair develops on the head. • More muscle tissue and bones have developed, and the bones become harder. • The fetus makes active movements. • Sucking motions are made with the mouth. • The liver and pancreas produce their appropriate fluid secretions.	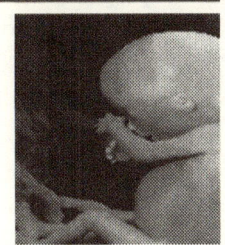
Five	• Eyebrows and lashes appear. • Nails appear on fingers and toes. • The fetus is more active with increased muscle development. • Quickening" usually occurs (the mother can feel the fetus moving). • Fetal heartbeat can be heard with a stethoscope.	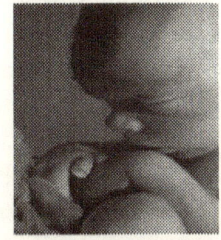
Six	• The fetus reaches a length of 11 or more inches. • All the eye components are developed. • Rapid brain development. • Eyelids open and close. • Babies born in the middle of the sixth month have a 10%–35% survival rate. • Babies born at the end of the sixth month have a 50%–80% survival rate.	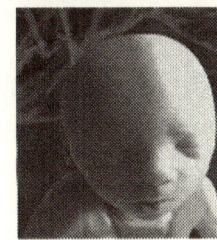

—Characteristics from Medline Plus, Medical Encyclopedia,
a service of the National Institutes of Health at
www.nlm.nih.gov/medlineplus/encyclopedia.html
—Images with permission from Priests for Life at
www.priestsforlife.org/images

I realize that pro-abortion groups respond angrily to the use of such images, claiming they are used only to inflame passions and should not be introduced in a civil discussion of abortion. I disagree completely. This line of argument is nothing more than another attempt by pro-abortion groups to continue the shell game. They want to keep the focus on choice and religious intolerance while steering people away from the real issue. These images of fetal development are not included to inflame. They are included because of their obvious relevance to the question of when life begins. It's easy to understand why pro-abortionists protest the use of fetal images in this debate. It's a lot easier to believe that a fetus is not a human life when it is out of sight and out of mind. While it might be easier on the conscience, it certainly is not intellectually honest to ignore what is scientifically known about fetal development.

These well established fetal characteristics and associated images also highlight once again the tremendous problem the Supreme Court created with the trimester-related abortion system. Can anyone looking at these characteristics and images today reach the conclusion that a fetus at 26 weeks differs significantly from a fetus at 27 weeks? Is there enough difference that one fetus should be protected from abortion and the other not? Progress in science has not been kind to advocates of abortion. I'm sure most hoped, and even expected, that advances in science would help undermine the faith-based belief that life begins at conception. After all, over the course of history, new scientific theories and discoveries have presented challenge after challenge to faith-based beliefs. In the case of abortion, just the opposite has occurred. The time at which a fetus can become a successful premature birth continues to move incrementally, but nevertheless relentlessly, in the direction of conception. At the same time, the ability of science to look inside the womb during the first and second trimesters presents us with images of fetal development that are far more advanced than previously imagined. This truly is a case of a picture being worth a thousand words. It's very hard to look at fetal images and not wonder how anyone could have the audacity to pretend to know when life begins. Fetal development is a continuous, incremental process that is too complex to parse into "pre-life" and "life" time segments. Science does not answer the question of when life begins, but it certainly has provided us with information that ought to cause us to carefully consider the folly of anyone who thinks they actually can answer that question.

The final source to consider is our own common sense. It might seem odd to appeal to something as ordinary as common sense, but we shouldn't be reluctant to do it. Common sense is at the very foundation of American values. Consider this from the Declaration of Independence:

> "We hold these truths to be **self-evident, t**hat all men are created equal; that they are endowed by their Creator with certain unalienable rights; that among these are life, liberty, and the pursuit of happiness; that, to secure these rights, governments are instituted among men, deriving their just powers from the governed….."

It wasn't law or science that informed the founders of America concerning the rights of man. To them it was self-evident, which is a very elegant way of saying it was common sense.

Common sense has played such a substantial role in the development of America that it would be quite accurate to say that we are a nation founded on common sense. Unburdened by history and tradition, and seeking to create a form of government never before known to man, the Founding Fathers had little they could draw on except noble aspirations and an uncommon abundance of common sense. They had no specific pattern of government to copy, only a world full of patterns to avoid. Common sense is evident throughout the system they developed: governmental checks and balances, freedom of the press, freedom of speech, freedom of worship, courts that assume innocence until guilt is proven, and so on. And American common sense did not end with the founders. It was the common sense of American pioneers migrating westward that allowed them to survive and thrive where law, science and other sources of wisdom were very scarce. That same common sense approach to life continues to this very day to be a hallmark of American culture. We shouldn't be hesitant about applying it on this issue.

So what would common sense tell us about when life begins? To start with we know life begins sometime between conception and an actual successful birth. At some point in that nine month cycle a fetus becomes an individual human life. So how do we determine where on the timeline to place a mark and say with confidence that on one side a fetus isn't life and on the other side it is? Let's start with the point at which the Court has decided life begins, week 27. Since the fetus can be delivered at that point and has a high likelihood of surviving, I'm certain nearly everyone would agree with the Court that any time beyond week 27 a fetus is considered human life. So at a minimum, we can initially agree to place the mark at week 27.

This has the effect of narrowing the timeline by one-third. We no longer have to be concerned with the third trimester because we have reached the conclusion that life clearly begins sometime between conception and 27 weeks. Why don't we just stop there and agree with the Court? To do so defies logic on two counts. First, as I have already shown, scientific advances have now made it possible for a child to be born and survive as early as week 22. So if viability of the fetus is our dividing line, we need to move the mark back five weeks from the current law.

Secondly, and more importantly in my mind, viability, which is defined by pro-abortionists as the ability of the fetus to survive a premature birth and live outside the womb, isn't a very common sense point at which to define when life begins. To say that a fetus is human life only if it can survive outside the womb is basing the definition of life on two things only: the level of dependency the child has on the mother, and whether or not we can see the child with our eyes, separate and distinct from the mother. As to the level of dependency on mother, a fetus in the womb is clearly 100 percent dependent on the mother for its existence. Oxygen, nourishment, warmth, comfort and all other needs of the fetus are provided through the physical connection with the mother. But is the life of a baby outside the womb any less dependent on the mother? With the exception of now being able to obtain oxygen directly from the air instead of through the mother's bloodstream, the baby still remains totally dependent on its mother to provide it with everything it was getting from her while in the womb. It's impossible for a baby to survive without the constant support of a parent, just as it's impossible for a fetus to survive in the womb without its mother.

So what then is viability? What is the difference between a totally dependent 7-month-old premature child and a 7-month-old fetus awaiting birth at or near its due date? Indeed, in terms of viability, what is the difference between a child one month after birth and a fetus awaiting delivery? There are really only two differences; 1) the baby takes in oxygen from the air, the fetus from the mother's bloodstream; 2) The baby is visible, the fetus is not. Yet look at how differently they are treated under current law and in the minds of anyone who thinks fetal viability determines when life begins. This inequality certainly can't be based on the fact that the baby breathes oxygen on its own. Newborns often require breathing assistance to survive. Nobody would ever think of withholding such support from a newborn child. Does a baby's initial inability to breathe on its own disqualify it from life? Of course not, so why should it disqualify an unborn fetus from life? Thus we are left with one possible conclusion. One factor alone separates baby viability and fetal viability—one is seen and the other is not. It's my own personal opinion that an out-of-sight, out-of-mind attitude is unfortunately the primary reason that Roe v. Wade has not been overturned.

I hope it's clear by now that using the traditional definition of viability to establish when life begins is not a reasonable approach. Clearly life in the womb is substantially developed at some point before it is able to leave the womb successfully. Common sense has now led us to the conclusion that life begins in the womb, sometime between conception and 22 weeks. Where do we go from here? One possibility would be to return to a practice introduced centuries ago that specified that life begins when the mother experiences discernable movement, for example kicking, in the womb. This first movement was thought to be caused by the spirit entering the fetus and was referred to as the "quickening" of the child. Though the time of quickening is very dependent on the individual fetus, in olden times it was generally believed to be between weeks 16 and 18. Or instead of choosing quickening as the time when life begins, perhaps we could look at the description of fetal characteristics on the previous pages and decide when a fetus has developed human characteristics that sufficiently qualify it to be called a human being. Or maybe we could look at the fetal images of the previous pages and determine in a similar manner when we think the fetus looks enough like life to call it that.

Or perhaps we should just admit that trying to specify when life begins is beyond our knowledge and capability. As one further illustration of the futility of any attempt to determine when life begins, suppose we choose to say that it begins precisely at the start of week 20. Does that mean one second earlier, life was not present? If we happen to be off by one second in our conclusion, we are making a tragic mistake. So we move the point backward one second in time and repeat the same question. Again we run the unacceptable risk of being off by one second. The fundamental problem is that we are trying to treat the development of life as a discreet series of steps when human development is not a discreet process—it's a continuous process. Life is not endowed in one discreet millisecond. It is acquired and enhanced through an extended period of time. Because there is not one specific definable step in the process that converts a non-living fetus into a living person, we are left with only our own personal opinion of when there is "enough life" present. Some might feel comfortable in making that determination, but I certainly wouldn't want my subjective opinion of when life begins to determine whether a child lives or dies.

So my own common sense leads me to the conclusion that we should just give in to the obvious and admit we are not able to determine when human life begins. It's beyond our capability to know for certain and tragically presumptive and arrogant to believe otherwise. Those who believe that abortion is wrong because life begins at conception are often accused of trying to impose their particular faith in God on others. In what has to be one of the greatest ironies of all time, those who believe that abortion is acceptable because a fetus is not a human life are making a judgment call that is beyond human capability to make. Their arrogance in assuming they know something that no human being can know actually puts them in the position of "playing God" on this issue. If those who think they are wise enough to play God are wrong, the practice of abortion is likely the greatest violation of human rights in history. The power over life and death is not something that should be granted to any individual or group of individuals, including prospective mothers and their doctors.

We should recognize our human limitations and admit we don't know when life begins. From conception to delivery, there is only one point in time that we can choose as the starting point for life and be sure we will never be wrong and that point is conception. There is no other common sense alternative. Imagine the colossal error if we choose any starting point after conception and then at a future point, find for any reason, that we ought to move that point back a little bit because of new understanding and knowledge. This is exactly the predicament the Court has put us in by defining the start of individual life as the point of viability outside the womb. Thirty years ago it was 27 weeks. Today, because of advances in medical science, it is closer to 22 weeks. In the meantime, because of the arrogance of a handful of justices, who incorrectly thought they knew when life begins, many thousands of viable children have been denied the right to life. It's a tragedy. Never, would we have allowed the life of even one newborn baby to be taken, and yet we have taken away the lives of many thousands of unseen, out-of-sight babies, who had a high likelihood of surviving outside the womb. No matter which point we might choose along the continuum from conception to birth, we are faced with the possibility of eventually being tragically wrong. There is only one point where we can be certain of not being wrong. That is the point of conception.

It's My Body

The most convincing arguments in support of abortion are based on the premise that every woman should be allowed to decide what she does with her own body, including whether or not she will maintain a pregnancy. A pregnancy is completely self-contained within her and places no burden on anyone other than the mother. And the mother's potential burden is substantial. She faces nine months of physical trauma and emotional challenge as the baby develops in her womb, followed by the even more daunting prospect of a lifetime commitment to nurture and support the child after birth. The consequences of proceeding with the pregnancy are enormous, life-changing and, perhaps, not at all desirable to the woman. It's her body. Shouldn't we let her choose what she does with it?

The argument for individual choice is very compelling, especially in a nation founded on the principles of freedom and individual rights. The early settlers of this country believed so strongly in these principles that they were willing to risk life, fortune and family to obtain them. That same respect for individual rights is as strong today as it was then. It's embedded in our DNA. Is it any wonder that individual choice is the most compelling argument for abortion? It's so compelling that savvy advocates of abortion have very wisely made it the central theme of their cause, describing themselves as pro-choice rather than pro-abortion. If abortion is pro-choice, what does that make anyone who is against abortion? By inference, they must be anti-choice. When put that way, it almost sounds like a person would have to be anti-American not to support abortion.

But putting immediate reactions aside, a more thoughtful consideration of the topic of individual rights reminds us that there are many compelling reasons to restrict an individual's right to choose. For example, we all understand that no man has the right to assault another with his fist. Why not? It's his body, his fist. Why can't he swing it into my nose if he wants? The reason this behavior is prohibited is obvious. We have probably all heard the well-worn phrase that describes this situation, "Your right to swing your fist ends where my nose begins." In the hierarchy of personal rights, we value protection from harm more than we value the freedom to swing a fist into another person's nose.

In this example, the two rights in question are separated by a wide margin in the hierarchy of individual freedom. On that list, swinging of fists doesn't get much respect. But what happens when the activity in question is high on the list of freedoms worth protecting? Consider another classic example, this one concerning freedom of speech. Can a woman exercise her freedom of speech in a theater? Probably not, even if all she wants to do is carry on a personal conversation with her companions. Chances are that any extended conversation will be an unacceptable distraction to others in the theater. They have paid for the right to see and hear the show and the woman's inconsiderate free speech is interfering with that right. She would likely receive a warning and eventually would be removed if she persisted with her "free speech."

These are two simplistic examples, but we could very easily prepare a list of hundreds, if not thousands, of additional examples, where we have collectively decided that not everything somebody wants to do should be allowed. Can a man rob a bank? Can a woman burn down a neighbor's house? Can a man steal another's car? The list could go on and on. But by now I hope this important fundamental point is made: Society has the right to restrict, and even eliminate individual behavior that harms another, harms self, or harms society in general. It's not difficult at all to restrict behavior when it has an obvious negative effect on another person. We tend to struggle more with the other two conditions—harm to self and harm to society in general. Though we have laws preventing the ultimate self-harm—suicide—we tend to give a lot of leeway to individuals bent on harming themselves, as long as innocent bystanders are not affected in any way. For example, alcoholism is in essence suicide in slow motion, but we have no laws to prevent it. We do of course intervene to stop self-destruction, but it's generally done out of compassion and not compelled by law.

Cases of individual actions harming society in general are the most difficult to resolve. It's not easy to assess how individual choices will impact society in general. Will it affect a large or small portion of the population? How grievous will the damage be? At times it's nearly impossible to predict what harms might be caused by a particular action and the effects on society might not become obvious until long after the initial act takes place. Nevertheless, societies have to make such determinations and here in the United States we have not shied away from making them. A significant number of the laws we live by are the result of our willingness to protect society in general from the commission of detrimental individual choice.

I've taken the time to walk through the previous examples to illustrate that there is a general framework for evaluating whether individual choice should be granted or restricted. And that framework can be utilized to put a woman's right to choose abortion to the test. First, let's run the right to choose argument through the "harm to another" test. If you have read the previous chapter, it will come as no surprise to you that I believe that in the act of abortion, the mother is not the only individual whose rights need to be considered. I am not going to rehash the entire chapter and if you missed it, I urge you to go back and read it. But for the sake of clarity, I offer just a brief reminder of the conclusions of the previous chapter: 1) I don't believe anyone can definitively say when life begins; and 2) Since we cannot know when life begins, the only safe and rational conclusion is to assume that life begins at conception. If life begins at conception, the mother isn't the only individual whose rights ought to be considered during pregnancy. When you compare the hierarchy of rights under consideration on each side of this equation, there is a tremendous gap in relative importance between the two. On one hand, the mother wants to assert her right to eliminate something from her life that is an inconvenience to her. Granted, this is not a small inconvenience. The effects of pregnancy are significant enough that they will certainly change her lifestyle and challenge her abilities for a good number of years to come. On the other hand, the developing child has a right to life itself. Unfortunately for the mother, there isn't any right she can assert—with the single exception being a threat to her own life—that trumps the primacy of the developing child's right to life. We not only have enacted laws to protect life, but as Americans we also live in a country where the value of life has been woven into the very fabric of our nation since its inception:

> "We hold these truths to be self-evident, that **all men are created equal; that they are endowed by their Creator with certain unalienable rights; that among these are life, liberty, and the pursuit of happiness**; that, to secure these rights, governments are instituted among men, deriving their just powers from the governed....."

The right to life is not open to fudging or negotiation in any way. It is an undeniable primary right. Period. End of sentence. The mother's right to choose must be superceded by the child's right to live. The life of another individual is far too steep a price to pay to eliminate even the sizeable inconvenience suffered by the mother in going forward with the pregnancy. Under these circumstances I believe the only logical and moral conclusion that can be reached is that a mother's right to choose ends when the life of the fetus begins.

I completely understand how cold and cruel this position might seem to any pregnant woman who really doesn't want to bear the significant burdens of pregnancy and child rearing. It must seem especially hard-hearted to some pregnant young women—perhaps still only girls—who arrived at this condition without fully understanding the long term consequences of potential pregnancy. As a father of six, I completely understand how difficult a mother's job is. I've seen it first hand, six times over. I have great sympathy for any woman who is pregnant and doesn't want the many challenges that come with pregnancy. So, how can I be so heartless? Why would I advocate that someone go through a life-altering event such as pregnancy against their will?

If you think seriously about it, all of us—not just me—are more than willing to consign a mother to these duties against her will. Once a child is out of the womb, all of us, whether pro-abortion or anti-abortion, agree that the mother cannot choose to ignore her responsibility to the child. We all agree she must provide for the child or suffer severe consequences. It doesn't matter to us if she doesn't want to do it; she has an obligation, and we are quite willing to hold her to it, even though we might be sympathetic to her burden. The rights of the child take precedence over the desires of the mother. The bottom line is that every one of us is willing to compel a mother to suffer the burdens of motherhood. The only disagreement arises over the time at which those burdens get locked-in. For abortion advocates, it's at birth. For the rest of us, it's either at conception or at some other point preceding birth. I don't point this out to indicate that I find personal comfort in the fact that all of us are willing to impose burdens on mothers. I do it to demonstrate how feeble the argument is that abortion is justified because we shouldn't impose motherhood on a pregnant woman who doesn't want it. Though we should have tremendous empathy for anyone in an unwanted pregnancy, I believe we are morally obligated to ensure that the pregnancy proceeds to completion. What else can we conclude when the result of abortion is to potentially take the life of another human being?

Anyone who is willing to concede that life begins at conception, or for that matter, at any point in the womb, would have to admit that abortion fails this first test. Therefore, based on this criterion alone, abortion can and should be restricted on the basis that it harms another individual. But the case against a woman's right to choose is strengthened considerably by consideration of the remaining two test conditions. Returning to the evaluation framework, let's now run this question through the "harm to self or to society" tests. Though there are rare cases of irreversible physical harm to women who undergo abortion, the same is true for completed pregnancies. So, I readily concede that physical harm to self is not a credible argument against abortion. In fact, when you look at abortion entirely from the perspective of the woman, it would seem that abortion not only doesn't harm her, it in fact makes her life better than it would have been if the pregnancy proceeded. Nine months of physical discomfort and many years of parental commitment are avoided. What possible self or societal harm is prevented by not allowing a woman the right to choose an abortion? Before answering that question, it's helpful to review the entire sequence of events that precede the choice to have an abortion.

Pro-choice advocates would like us to believe that a woman's right to choose boils down to one choice and one choice only: the choice to terminate a pregnancy. However, a woman makes many choices before arriving at a point where choosing abortion is even possible, let alone a right. And for each of the many choices made prior to pregnancy, nearly everyone supports a woman's right to choose. Putting aside the case of rape until later, every woman has the choice of whether or not to be with a man. She has the choice of whether or not to remove her clothing. She has the choice of whether or not to use birth control. She may or may not have some influence in the man's choice to use birth control. And she may or may not have the choice to stop the act before it has produced a possible pregnancy. By the time a pregnancy occurs the woman has already exercised her right to choose what she does with her own body several times.

We often forget, or perhaps we choose to ignore the fact, that the right to choose is always accompanied by the obligation to assume responsibility for the consequences of our choices. It's human nature to enjoy the good consequences and attempt to evade the bad ones. Unwanted pregnancy is a perfect illustration of this all-too-human tendency. Every one of the choices that lead up to conception is desirable in the eyes of both participants. In fact, the very reason those choices are made in the first place is to experience those desirable consequences. Both participants know full well that the last choice in this series of enjoyable choices could result in pregnancy. But when that possibility becomes a reality, instead of accepting responsibility for their choices, the participants avoid accountability by claiming the right to make yet another choice that will neatly remove the consequences of their previous actions. In this sense, abortion is unfortunately a "fix"—an act designed to "undo" a choice that produced undesirable consequences. In this light, those who couch the pro-abortion argument in terms of pro-choice rhetoric are ultimately just diverting attention from an act of personal irresponsibility.

I believe such evasion of responsibility is very detrimental to individual character, and its cumulative long-term effects are also detrimental to society. The impact is impossible to measure and quantify, but consider your own experience with this problem. I think we have all come in contact with increasing numbers of people who seek to avoid accountability for their choices and actions. Perhaps it's a student who fails a class and blames it on poor instruction rather than his or her own lack of effort. Perhaps it's a colleague at work who is fired for excessive absence and sues the company for age discrimination. Perhaps it's the neighbor who spends well beyond his means and then declares personal bankruptcy to avoid his obligations to creditors. Perhaps it's the crook who believes that his criminal behavior is the result of poor parenting. How about that relatively recent twist in American culture? In just a few decades we've gone from "the devil made me do it" to "my parents made me do it." That doesn't sound like progress to me.

Rather than make a futile effort to quantify the negative impact of this all-too-common phenomenon, I would simply ask you to consider whether or not your own experience leads you to believe that this attitude is harmful to individuals and to society in general. I'm confident you will agree with the premise that American society is headed in the wrong direction if acceptance of irresponsibility is on the rise. And there is no doubt in my mind that acceptance of irresponsibility is growing at an alarming rate. If you think this is a minor concern, think about the fact that we recently had a president, Bill Clinton, whose relationship with "that woman—Ms. Lewinsky," exposed more than Clinton's sexual appetite and irresponsibility—it also exposed the willingness of many Americans to tolerate deception and out-right lying as acceptable behavior. It was bad enough that the president of the United States—the most powerful and visible representative of American values in the world—was embroiled in this salacious drama. But even more disturbing was the fact that after his lies were exposed, many of his supporters were unfazed. The willingness of a significant number of Americans to brush-it-off and let-it-go was mind boggling. The attitude of irresponsibility in our country has become so common that we no longer expect even our presidents, let alone our neighbors, to take responsibility for their actions.

This kind of behavior is symptomatic of an underlying erosion of a fundamental American value. It's a very serious problem. There is nothing more fundamental to the American way of life than freedom of choice. But a system founded on choice cannot be sustained unless the companion of choice—accountability—is maintained. These two principles are opposite sides of the same coin. If accountability is diminished, it's inevitable that freedom of choice will follow suit. Accountability is the governor on the engine of choice. When people know they will be held accountable for choices, there is a significant disincentive for undesirable behavior. Society can only maintain an acceptable level of order and protect the common good if undesirable behavior is kept at a tolerable level. If personal accountability declines significantly, and we do nothing to reverse that trend, we will eventually reach the point where the order of society is threatened. When that point is reached, there are really only two ways for society to maintain acceptable order. One way is to increase significantly the "policing mechanisms" of the state to force a necessary level of accountability. In essence, this would be controlling the problem by managing it from the backend. The other way to deal with it would be a front-end fix: limit the number of choices people can make on their own—in other words, if people are unable to make good choices on their own, take away their right to choose. Both of these solutions are undesirable. A backend solution produces a society in which good choices are in essence compelled by the state and not by the conscience of its citizens. On the other hand, a front-end solution can eventually destroy the very foundation of American culture by eliminating one of our founding principles—freedom of choice. If we don't take action to restore individual accountability to its rightful place as the price we must pay for free choice, we will someday be living in an America quite different from the country envisioned by our founders and admired by the world.

I don't mean to imply that the practice of abortion is the most significant contributor to this slide down the slippery slope of diminishing personal accountability. However, it is one of many contributing factors. Likewise, I'm not attempting to analyze our society's drift toward irresponsibility in any respectable depth. It goes beyond the scope and objectives of this book and deserves a thorough airing elsewhere. I'm only attempting to point out that the path to abortion is often lined with many choices that are not matched with the requisite accountability. But reckless decision making alone doesn't cover the full extent of the irresponsibility of abortion. The availability of abortion actually serves as an incentive for irresponsibility. Don't you think that men and women would more carefully consider their sexual choices if they knew that abortion wouldn't be there to bail them out in the end? The fact that abortion is available has certainly increased the level of irresponsible behavior. If you have any doubt, consider the recent remarks of popular comedian and 2005 Oscar host Chris Rock:

> Shock Oscar host Chris Rock recently declared that abortion in the United States is a "beautiful thing!" "Abortion, it's beautiful, it's beautiful abortion is legal. I love going to an abortion rally to pick up women, cause you know they are (willing to have intercourse)," Rock said during his club routine.

—From the Drudgereport, February 15, 2005

It's easy to dismiss Rock's comments as an expression of bad taste in search of a laugh, but there is no doubt in my mind that his remarks accurately reflect the obvious fact that sexual intercourse is more freely practiced when accountability for pregnancy can so easily be annulled.

This lack of accountability runs 180 degrees counter to the principles that are at the foundation of American culture. As a society, we should not be shy about preserving the fundamental values of our culture. Our entire system of government and law is built on these principles. I wouldn't go so far as to say that, "A house divided against itself cannot stand," but it should be obvious to everyone, that our American house is losing some of its value as parts of the structure are drifting out of alignment with the foundation.

I think we would all agree that accountability is an important companion of choice. But does society have the right to enforce individual accountability on those who would rather escape it? We certainly do. If a driver exceeds the speed limit, a fine is imposed. If a robber takes money from a bank, he goes to jail. If a serial killer is apprehended, he will likely face a death sentence. The list is endless. Our vast legal system is engaged primarily in the business of enforcing accountability as a consequence of personal choice. Why then are we so reluctant to require accountability in pregnancy? I think it has to do with the fact that pregnancy is the result of a universal human desire, common to all of us. We don't all want to rob banks, but almost all of us desire sexual interaction. We have great sympathy for those who have made the choices leading up to pregnancy because we have all "been there" to one degree or another. And it often happens so early in life. Perhaps, even to our own children when they are yet too young to understand fully the consequences of the choices they are making. The consequences are so significant that the entire trajectory of life is changed. Dreams can be shattered and potential unrealized.

Yet, though we have tremendous empathy for anyone in an unwanted pregnancy, I believe we are morally obligated to ensure that the pregnancy proceeds to completion. When put to the tests of harm to others, harm to self and harm to society in general, abortion looses on all three counts. What else can we conclude when abortion is potentially taking the life of another? What else can we conclude when the practice of abortion encourages irresponsible behavior? Making abortion illegal is not taking away a woman's right to choose. She still has the right to choose from a lengthy list of activities with men, ranging widely from platonic to completely intimate. But if she chooses to have sexual intercourse without effective birth control, she must take responsibility for the consequences of that choice. Instead of focusing on "fixing the problem pregnancy" after it arrives, we need to focus our efforts on preventing the problem pregnancy from ever arriving. Much greater emphasis needs to be placed on educating men and women on the severity of the potential consequences of engaging in intimate relations. At present, exactly the reverse is happening. Our culture emphasizes the importance of sex, glamorizing it at every turn, and downplays its consequences by allowing, and in some cases encouraging, abortion to fix the problem. How could we have it so backwards?

I'll end this chapter by returning to the difficult topic of rape and incest. Pregnancies of this nature are clearly a different story. There is a strong temptation on my part to conclude that a victim of a non-consensual pregnancy should be allowed to extricate themselves from the situation through abortion. However, to be consistent, I cannot. Once having concluded that an individual life is at stake in the womb, it's not possible to go there. The only exception I can consistently support is in the case of a mother's life being at risk, which would be analogous to self-defense. It's true that a rape victim has a terrible burden to carry for something she did not bring on herself. Asking her to proceed with the pregnancy extends this burden several months and in the end may have long-lasting negative effects that abortion could avoid. But two wrongs don't make a right. I believe for the sake of protecting potential life we should focus our efforts on punishing the sexual criminal to the fullest extent possible. We shouldn't compound the damage by allowing an abortion to alleviate some of the victim's suffering. Indeed, making abortion illegal to protect an individual life provides a solid rationale for strengthening the criminal sanctions against rape. Sentences for convicted rapists should be strengthened to the same levels of punishment that apply to other criminal activities that impact the life or quality of life of another individual. For the victim, we should provide the fullest level of counseling and medical support we can provide and hope that the victim's life will not be irretrievably damaged by the actions of a criminal.

Unwanted and Defective Birth

The two previous chapters addressed the issue of whether or not abortion ought to be considered a personal right. In this chapter, the discussion will focus on the reasons most often given for exercising that right. These reasons include:

- Birth defects are identified in the fetus that will likely cause the child to be handicapped.

- The parent(s) do not desire a child at this time.

- The parent(s) might desire a child, but are financially or otherwise unfit to provide the child with proper care.

Not surprisingly, the reasons for having an abortion are always expressed in the best possible light, similar to the way in which the pro-choice label has been used so effectively in positioning abortion as a woman's right to choose. All three reasons outlined above can be put quite conveniently in the context of having an abortion "for the good of the child." Those who make this argument say that abortion isn't occurring because the parents are irresponsible or selfish. It's being done because abortion is in the best interest of the unborn child. In other words, it's selfless, not selfish. It's a difficult task to persuade anyone that a selfless act to spare a child from misery is a bad thing. While this argument does have the effect of putting the abortion decision in the best possible light, we should not allow that light to distract us from the significant moral inconsistencies that arise from a decision to terminate a pregnancy for these reasons.

Let's examine each of these three reasons in turn. The first concerns the physical condition of the developing child. Advances in medical knowledge and technology now allow doctors to predict birth defects with reasonable accuracy. Parents can know, often relatively early in the pregnancy, if their child will be born with a handicap. Physical and mental deficiencies of many types can be identified, and a determination can be made to abort the pregnancy before the child is exposed to the challenges of life presented by the particular handicap. Knowing the difficulties these children will surely face, aren't the parents doing a good thing in terminating what would likely be an extremely difficult existence?

On the surface, it sounds like the humane thing to do. However, on deeper examination, it's a practice completely at odds with the values and laws we have adopted to protect handicapped individuals. It's impossible to reconcile the moral and logical inconsistency of doing everything possible to ensure that a handicapped baby's life is sustained on the one hand, and on the other, allowing—sometimes even encouraging—the abortion of a handicapped fetus. As an example of the moral and logical inconsistency this practice introduces, consider a child born blind. Once the blind baby is out of the womb, we would never allow that child's life to be terminated in order to spare it from the hardship of a sightless life. Such a thing is just plain unthinkable. You can substitute any physical or mental impairment for blindness, and the conclusion is always the same. We value and respect life so much that we would never terminate it, no matter the degree of impairment. And this doesn't apply to infant life only. We are just as adamant about the protection given to handicapped seniors. In spite of widely publicized recent debate on this issue, we do not allow anyone to take the life of someone suffering from Alzheimer's or any other incapacitating ailment in order to save the sufferer from a less than perfect existence. In spite of the impairment and the difficulties created by it, we let life play-out without interference. The only difference between the handicapped baby in our arms and the handicapped fetus in a mother's womb is location. One is in a location we can see. The other is out of sight. Preventing a handicapped birth through abortion is the moral and logical equivalent of allowing parents of handicapped children to gather those children on a leaking boat, allowing them to push the boat out to sea where it will surely sink, drowning all of the children, and then allowing them to claim it was done for humanitarian reasons. It is, of course, absurd to even consider it.

I realize that taking this stand means that many more handicapped children would be born into circumstances that are not only less than ideal, but are also extremely difficult for the parents, extended family and friends. It's tempting at this point to look at the most positive possible outcomes of handicapped birth by reviewing a list of famous people, handicapped at birth, who have made tremendous contributions to society. An impressive list could be compiled to point out what the world might have missed without the lives of such people. But for every handicapped person we might put on such a list, I am sure we could also compile another list, probably longer, of those whose birth defects have consigned them to a very difficult existence with little in the way of accomplishment to show for it. We are all likely acquainted with some sad personal experience in this regard. So to be honest, we must recognize that we are not able to provide productive lives for many who are born with birth defects. There are some cases where the imperfections detected in the womb are so pronounced, so obvious, and so devastating, that even I could accept that abortion could be performed. In my own experience, I have heard of babies in the womb not having necessary organs or other physical attributes that would make life outside the womb impossible or nearly so. If the evidence is overwhelming, I have no problem with parents and doctors together reaching the conclusion that terminating the pregnancy is the right thing to do.

However, for less than life-threatening defects, we need to be consistent and allow life, even in a diminished way, to proceed. In some cases, the child will have a wonderful life. In other cases the child will not. Some will die at birth, others shortly thereafter. Still others will live long, unproductive and painful lives. In spite of the possible outcomes, we ought to protect the right to life of any child in the womb, just as we protect the life of every existing handicapped person. It may well be that in retrospect the child will be grateful for any form of life, as imperfect as it might be. It might also be that the child would have chosen not to proceed with life. The point is that we will never know the desires of an unborn child. Therefore, we must err on the side of providing access to life; and let the chips fall where they may. Quite often, the greatest benefits of a handicapped birth come to the parents, family and friends of the child. They learn selflessness, patience, love, dignity and many other worthwhile virtues while supporting their loved-one through life's challenges. Great good can come to many from such a humble source. It's best we let all viable life proceed and not make the mistake of determining someone else's fate for them.

Though I've drawn the conclusion that we shouldn't abort children to prevent birth defects, it is at least a weighty enough moral dilemma to consider. And though I dismiss it, I don't do so lightly. The other two reasons given for abortion—parents not desiring a child at the present time, or parents who might desire a child but are unable to provide proper care—don't reach the same level of credibility. The two are fundamentally the same. A mother alone, or in consultation with others, has decided that a proper home environment cannot be provided for the baby. Perhaps there are insufficient financial resources. Perhaps the parents are physically unable to parent a child. Perhaps the mother is a teenager, not yet emotionally mature enough to support a child. Or, least convincing of all, perhaps the parents just don't want children in their lives right now.

In all such cases, I actually agree with the determination that the child should not be born to parents who are unwilling or unable to provide properly for the child. But taking the child's life through abortion is not the solution. In fact, abortions performed for this reason are completely at odds with the values and laws we apply in the protection of unwanted or inadequately supported children. For example, consider what happens when a hopelessly addicted mother gives birth and is unable to properly care for the child. We have wisely created entire agencies whose function is to discover such instances of child neglect or abuse. Once the threat to the well-being of the child is discovered, would we ever decide that the appropriate remedy to alleviate the neglect is to take the life of the child? No. We would consider anyone who thought this way crazy, and if they acted on the thought, we would consider them criminal. Instead, we do the right thing and demand that the parent correct the problem. And if the parent doesn't correct the problem, we remove the child from the parent and find a suitable home for the child through foster care or adoption. Taking any approach that would further harm the child is unthinkable. Just as in the example cited at the beginning of this chapter, the only difference between a neglected child in a bad home environment and an unwanted fetus in a mother's womb is location. One is in a location we can see, the other is out of sight. Having an abortion to prevent the birth of an unwanted or unsupportable child is a far more tenuous argument then even the case of abortion for children with potential birth defects. And the same analogy is just as applicable in this case. Allowing abortion to prevent the birth of an unwanted or unsupportable child is the moral and logical equivalent of allowing parents of unwanted or abused children to gather those children together on a leaking boat, pushing the boat out to sea and allowing it to sink, drowning all of the children and then claiming it was done for humanitarian reasons. The unwanted or unsupportable child should be taken from the parent at birth and placed in a foster home or with adoptive parents who can provide adequately for the support of the child.

This obviously places quite a burden on society to provide first-class foster care and adoptive services for the placement of unwanted children. We should do it, no matter the cost. I don't pretend to know how good or bad the systems supporting adoption and foster care in our country are presently. I've never had the occasion to use them or come in contact with them in any way. If someone wants to argue that they are inadequate for the task at hand, I wouldn't attempt to refute the argument. I would only say that if the system is inadequate, we must fix the system. It certainly should be no excuse for terminating a pregnancy. This is the equivalent of saying we ought to terminate cancer patients because there is a shortage of cancer treatment facilities to accommodate them.

Though at first consideration it might seem to be selfless and admirable to prevent a child from being born into less than desirable circumstances, it doesn't stand the test of deeper examination. It's completely at odds with the values and laws we have established to protect all viable life and provide that life with a proper and supportive environment. Never would our basic principles tolerate taking the life of an indigent child to remove him or her from poverty. Never would we take the life of a child whose parents no longer want to make the effort to care for them. Never would we take the life of a physically or mentally handicapped child to ease their difficult life. Why? Because we believe that everyone is entitled to life, no matter the conditions under which it might be lived. The only person who can determine if a challenging life is worth living is the person who will live that life. And there is plenty of evidence in the millions of people who live in difficult circumstances that no matter the degree of difficulty the desire for life wins out over the alternative.

Everybody's Doing It

There are many who argue that we ought to allow abortion because the most "sophisticated" and "civilized" nations of the world allow it. Banning abortion would make us appear backward and perhaps even "third world" to our intelligent and sophisticated friends around the globe. Abortion is an important symbol of our cultural maturity and is required to maintain our position among the sophisticated and civilized nations of the world.

In response to this argument, I have a brief and politically incorrect counterargument: Just because someone else is doing it, doesn't make it right.

Especially if the "someone else" is Western Europe—and for Americans it most often is. Many of our ancestors left Western Europe, primarily to escape the suppression of human capability and dignity that was the consequence of the European belief that all men were not created equal. These first Americans fled political systems in which an individual's place in society and opportunities in life were predetermined by birthright. A baby in the womb of a peasant was considered a lower form of life than a baby in the womb of a land owner. And even the baby of a land owner was considered a lower form of life than a baby born into royalty. Our ancestors believed just the opposite—every baby enters life on equal footing with everyone else. The difference couldn't be spelled out any more clearly than it is in the Declaration of Independence: We hold these truths to be self-evident, that all men are created equal. On the issue of individual rights, most especially birthright, emulating the practices of Western

Europe would most certainly cause our forefathers to spin in their graves. In fact, this is the one subject that would probably cause them to spin so fast they would spontaneously combust.

Though I think this counterargument is sufficient in and of itself as a rebuttal, research on the topic revealed some very interesting information concerning our place in the world relative to abortion practice. It was quite an eye opener for me (and it was enough of an eye opener that I am going to shift gears and not return to my original line of thinking until later in the chapter). I had fully expected that a review of European abortion law and practice would confirm my expectations that Europe is more liberal than the United States in both. To my great surprise, I found that nearly all countries in Europe are more restrictive in law and more conservative in practice than we are. While not a comprehensive list of abortion practice in Europe, this representative sample makes the point:

- Abortion not legal: Ireland, Poland, Portugal, Spain, Switzerland

- Abortion only in first trimester: Austria, Czech Republic, France, Italy

- Abortion only in first and second trimester: United Kingdom

- Abortion any time: Denmark, Germany, Greece, Netherlands, Norway, Sweden

As always, it's a little more complicated than a simple chart can indicate. For example, abortion in France beyond the first trimester is allowed for protection of the mother's health, cases of rape, and potential birth defects. And theoretically abortion in the second trimester is restricted in the United Kingdom, though abortion is allowed through the second trimester for a variety of reasons, up to and including socio-economic reasons. In actual practice, the many exceptions to the law in the U.K. allow abortion on demand any time prior to the third trimester.

Where does the United States fit in this comparison? At first glance it might seem that we are aligned with the United Kingdom, allowing abortion only in the first and second trimesters of pregnancy. But that would not be accurate. Even though Roe v. Wade theoretically limits abortion in the third trimester, the Court provided a loophole that is on occasion utilized to justify an abortion at that late stage of pregnancy. Specifically, the Court ruled that in the third trimester states may regulate abortion to protect fetal life, but not at the expense of the woman's life or health. Few would argue with an abortion that is required to save the mother's life. Though not every mother would choose this option, it is the logical equivalent of taking the life of the fetus in "self defense." I believe it is a necessary and advisable loophole. The second component of the loophole is another story. Threats to a woman's health are not nearly as black and white as threats to her life. It can be difficult to determine when a threat to a woman's health is a serious threat or a convenient excuse for an abortion. Especially with the increased emphasis on issues of mental health which can be far more difficult to discern than issues of physical health. Though relatively rare when compared to instances of abortion in the first and second trimesters, third trimester abortions are performed in the United States even when the life of the mother is not seriously at risk. This practice positions us at some point between the practices of the United Kingdom and the practices of the most liberal countries of Europe. There are additional nuances for other countries listed, but the overall conclusion is still the same—abortion law in most of the countries of Western Europe is more restrictive than abortion law in the United States. Even France, the most often sited example of cultural sophistication, is more restrictive than we are.

The levels at which abortion is actually practiced in Europe are also enlightening. Consider the following table which shows the percentage of total pregnancies terminated by abortion, ranked from most frequent to least:

- Sweden   26%
- Czech Republic   25%
- United Kingdom   22%
- France   21%
- Norway   20%
- Denmark   19%
- Italy   19%
- Germany   15%
- Spain   15%
- Switzerland   14%
- Netherlands   13%
- Greece   11%
- Austria   3%
- Portugal   0.3%
- Poland   0.05%

—2004 by Wm. Robert Johnston, www.johnstonsarchive.net/
policy/abortion/wrjp333pd.html

What would you guess the number to be in the United States?
Would it surprise you to know that it's around 25 percent? That puts
us with Sweden and the Czech Republic at the top of the list. And the
countries with us at the top have small populations relative to the
United States. In absolute numbers, the United States is the overwhelming leader in abortion among "sophisticated" nations. No
country in Europe is even close.

My research also dispelled another misconception. I had assumed
that legal abortion was available in Europe long before it was available
in the United States. Sadly, the fact is that the United States was actu-

ally on the forefront of legalized abortion. Nearly all of the European countries legalized abortion a few years after the Roe v. Wade decision was handed down in the United States. They were following our lead. That makes the argument that we ought to allow abortion because Western Europe does a circular argument. We weren't following anyone. They were following us.

That's the overview of the Western World. What about abortion law and practice in the rest of the world? I would summarize abortion practices in the various regions of the world as follows, from the highest level of incidence to the lowest:

- China and North Korea not only allow abortion on demand at any point in a pregnancy, but actually require it in some cases as a form of population control. They are by far the most liberal nations in abortion law and practice in the world.

- Russia, Ukraine and several of the former satellite countries of the Soviet Union allow abortion on demand through the first two trimesters. Legally most have restrictions on late term abortion, but the percentage of abortions performed compared to potential births is near the 50 percent range, which is astounding. That's more than twice the rate of the United States.

- United States as already discussed.

- The majority of Western Europe as already discussed

- Africa is a mixed bag, with practices in some countries consistent with those of Europe and other countries imposing total bans.

- Central and South America are almost entirely against abortion.

- The majority of the rest of the world is against legal abortion with a few pockets here and there of restricted abortion.

So there it is in black and white. The only two regions in the world with more liberal views on abortion than the United States are the two centers of Communism. In fact, though we are thankfully far behind the level of practice in Communist China, we are arguably closer to the practice of Russia than we are to Western Europe. And we are way out on a limb when compared with our neighbors in this hemisphere.

This worldwide mosaic of abortion practice makes a lot of sense when you consider the extent to which various cultures around the world value individual rights. Under communism, individuals are subservient to the state. Individuals are nothing more than cogs in a big wheel. With that philosophy, it comes as no surprise that protection of life, whether in the womb or out, is not a priority. At the other extreme, Central and South America are predominantly of the Catholic faith, which teaches that every individual is important in the eyes of God. It's no surprise that protection of life is important public policy in these countries. In between these two extremes is Western Europe. That too should come as no surprise. Europe, since the period of the Enlightenment in the 15th century has struggled to balance religious faith and secular ideals, most often ending up at some point between the two. European abortion practice clearly follows that pattern. Abortion is generally allowed while the fetus is considered not "close enough to life" to be viable outside the womb and banned after viability is reached. In general, both religious and secular Europeans are quite satisfied with the compromise.

In each of these examples, it's clear to see that the practice of abortion in any nation is commensurate with the level to which individual rights is important to that particular culture. The greater the level of respect for individual rights, the less abortion is practiced. However, there is one glaring exception to this rule—the United States of America. Quite frankly our place on this chart makes absolutely no logical sense given our cultural values. We, of all the nations of the world, believe most strongly in the principles of individual rights, human equality and the inherent worth of individuals. We not only believe these principles, but our country was founded on them. This brings me full circle, returning to the premise with which I began this chapter. I think our Founding Fathers would be appalled that we have strayed so far from our roots. Abortion does not promote and protect individual rights, it devalues and denies them. On all other fronts, we continue to be the role model to the world for protection of human rights and equal opportunity for everyone. But we find that our tolerance for, and even support of, abortion rights aligns us more with the forces in the world that would deny human rights than with our own founding principles. It isn't the kind of company we should keep.

Guns

The intensity of the abortion debate hasn't diminished at all in the decades following Roe v. Wade. The issue is a permanent political fixture. Gun control on the other hand, is an issue that fades in and out of the public conscience. Its relevance at any point in time is determined by the magnitude and frequency of tragic events caused by the misuse of firearms. Public reaction to such tragedies is often initially intense, but the outrage usually dissipates rapidly. Two relatively recent events are an exception to that rule—the assassination attempt on President Ronald Reagan in 1981, and the student massacre at Columbine High School in 1998.

On March 30, 1981, President Reagan delivered a speech at the Washington Hilton Hotel to members of the National Conference of the Building and Construction Trades Department of the AFL-CIO. He left the hotel through a rear service entrance for a short walk to the motorcade that would return him to the White House. John W. Hinckley, Jr. was in the small crowd behind the hotel. He stepped forward and fired several shots at President Reagan with a .22-caliber handgun. Four men were wounded in the shooting—President Reagan, Secret Service Agent Timothy McCarthy, Washington, D.C. police officer Thomas Delahanty and Reagan's Press Secretary, James Brady. For those of us who had only recently moved beyond the discouragingly violent decade of the 1960's, this attempt resurrected memories of the fatal assassinations of John Kennedy, Robert Kennedy and Martin Luther King. It was especially disheartening that it happened to President Reagan. He had campaigned on a platform of optimism and hope and his administration was off to a good start restoring public confidence after two decades of confidence-shattering turmoil. The attempt on Reagan's life brought back discouraging memories not only of the previous assassinations, but of Vietnam, Watergate and the ineffectiveness of the Carter years, memories which we hoped were finally relegated to obscurity. Fortunately, it turned out to be an unsuccessful and isolated incident, and in his two terms in office, President Reagan successfully reinvigorated the American optimism he embodied.

Though President Reagan, Timothy McCarthy and Thomas Delahanty all recovered fully from their wounds, James Brady was not so fortunate. Brain damage from a serious head wound left him partially paralyzed for life. Brady was unable to continue as Press Secretary in the Reagan administration, though he maintained the title of Press Secretary throughout both of Reagan's terms. Brady and his wife, Sarah, decided to make the best of their misfortune, leading an effort to pass gun control legislation in the hope it would prevent similar injury to others. Because of their leadership and considerable public support for reform, in 1993 the Brady Handgun Violence and Protection Act, or Brady Bill, was passed by Congress. To this day, the Brady's continue to pursue even tighter controls on the sale of firearms.

The Brady Bill is practical legislation. The law requires that registered firearm dealers complete two checks before a purchase is completed. First, the purchaser must produce valid personal identification and second, the seller must check an FBI database to ensure the purchaser is not the subject of any current or prior criminal investigation that would disqualify the purchaser from owning a gun. The purchasing process mandated by the Brady Bill is very reasonable and does not cause any significant delay in purchasing a handgun. As long as the buyer has valid identification and is not on the FBI's criminal database, there is no problem. Anyone who is legally eligible to own a firearm will not be hindered in any way from obtaining it. With adequate identification and a good record, only a few minutes is added to the purchase process. It's a small price to pay to make it more difficult for criminals to obtain handguns; although, I'm sure it doesn't stop them. A criminal who is serious about acquiring a gun will likely not encounter much difficulty in finding one on the black market. But at least we have some assurance that the firearm acquisition process for criminals isn't as simple as going to the local gun shop.

In spite of the obvious common sense of the Brady Bill and its minor imposition on legal buyers and legitimate sellers, it was excruciatingly difficult to push through Congress. It would be easier to understand a reluctance to require identity checks when purchasing handguns if identity checks in American society were a rare requirement. But what the Brady Bill adds to the handgun purchase process is analogous to what we all experience when purchasing even the most mundane items with a credit card. We are required to show identification as the clerk scans our credit card to determine if we have sufficient funds to cover the purchase. It's a two step process—1) validate identification, and 2) confirm credit worthiness. Likewise, under the Brady Bill, a handgun purchase requires two steps—1) validate identification, and 2) confirm the buyer is not a criminal. Yet it took more than a decade of lobbying by the Brady's, and an army of supporters, to achieve this very modest victory. That's right, an entire decade of struggle to ensure that registered handgun dealers do not sell handguns to known criminals. This will give you some indication of the strength of the forces opposing gun control legislation.

The Columbine High School massacre occurred on April 20, 1999 near Littleton, Colorado. Eric Harris and Dylan Klebold, students at the school, arrived that day armed to the teeth with guns, home-made bombs and deadly hatred. They murdered 12 fellow students and one teacher before ending the terror by committing suicide. Twenty-four others were injured in the rampage. Harris and Klebold were armed with a semi-automatic handgun, two sawed-off shotguns and nearly 100 home-made bombs. The lion's share of the carnage was inflicted by gunfire from weapons that were acquired through illegal means. The original buyers—acquaintances of Harris and Klebold—had the legal right to purchase the weapons for personal use, but illegally turned them over to the killers. The two juveniles could not have legally acquired the guns without this assistance. In essence, the purchasers were aiding in the illegal acquisition of the firearms in much the same way teenagers would solicit friends of legal age to purchase alcohol for them. The pair who purchased the handgun was found guilty of illegally transferring the gun and received prison terms. The owner of the rifle and two shotguns was not charged for the violation.

The Columbine massacre stunned us. News crews were on the scene as the deadly event unfolded, and in-depth coverage monopolized the media for weeks. There have been many shooting incidents in schools both before and since Columbine, but the scope and scale of this tragedy exceeded any other and captured the attention of the entire nation. In the hope that future massacres could be avoided, a significant effort has been made to understand the motives and means that fueled this disaster. It is widely believed that Harris and Klebold's primary motive was revenge for "bullying" and humiliation suffered at the hands of fellow students at Columbine. In response to this discovery, schools all over the nation rapidly implemented "zero tolerance" rules to eliminate bullying. As for the means, the pair's ability to illegally acquire firearms and smuggle them into Columbine High School, turned an unfulfilled motive into a tragically fulfilled act. Again, schools across the nation acted rapidly, implementing zero tolerance rules for firearm possession. Zero tolerance rules are exactly what you would expect them to be. Without question or second guessing, school officials can expel students from school when they engage in bullying or are found with firearms anywhere near school property. School boards and administrators deserve great credit for the rapid implementation of these protective measures. It's impossible to know for certain if other Columbines have been prevented, but we are all familiar with stories of how zero tolerance policies have stopped bullying and removed firearms from students. It's most likely that serious problems have been avoided.

Preventative measures outside the public school system have been more difficult to identify and even more difficult to implement. In the aftermath of Columbine, there was a significant and sustained public outcry for strengthening gun control laws that might keep firearms out of the hands of deranged individuals like Harris and Klebold. Sadly, no significant change has been implemented. This lack of success, in spite of significant effort, is again an indication of the strength and effectiveness of the opposition to gun control. Indications are that it's even stronger today than it was at the time of the Reagan assassination attempt two decades ago. Supporters of the Brady Bill were at least able to get something passed. The Columbine massacre was much more devastating. And in spite of considerable effort to enact legislation that would make future Columbines less likely, the same processes are in place today as at the time of the disaster. The same loopholes that Harris and Klebold navigated to obtain firearms could be utilized again.

The political strength and influence of those who oppose gun control legislation is substantial and should not be underestimated. What is the source of this power? A recent gun ownership poll sheds some light on this question:

Gun Ownership:

- Percentage of all adult Americans owning a gun   40%

- Percentage of adults in each political affiliation owning a gun

   - Republicans   53%

   - Democrats   31%

   - Independents   36%

- For gun owners, average number of guns owned   4.4

- For total US adult population, average owned   1.7

Does Having a Gun in the House Make You Safer?

- Yes   42%

- No, more dangerous   46%

—Gallup Poll, January 4, 2005

The numbers are very revealing. Only 40 percent of adult Americans own firearms. That leaves a majority, 60 percent, who do not. In this era of razor-thin red and blue political margins, 60 percent is a sizeable majority. The poll also indicates that nearly half of us believe that having a firearm in the home makes it a more dangerous place, not a more protected place. This is just the opposite of what the anti-gun control forces preach. Finally, the poll indicates that even though only 40 percent of us own firearms that 40 percent is into serious ownership, averaging 4.4 guns per person. In total, the 40 percent minority who own guns possess an arsenal of weapons large enough to equip every adult in the country with 1.7 guns.

That's a lot of firepower. It provides some insight into why advocacy of gun ownership is so powerful. If someone is in favor of unrestricted private ownership of firearms, they tend to be strongly in favor of the proposition. There is no lukewarm support from gun owners when it comes to owning guns. They are a very dedicated minority. On the other hand, those of us who do not own firearms are not as passionate in our opposition. Even though we might believe that gun ownership has many potentially detrimental effects on society, we are reluctant to pursue restrictions. As is our American nature, we are willing to sacrifice a considerable amount of common good to preserve individual rights.

Is it worth it in this case? It probably was a valid trade-off in times past, but advances in weapon capability coupled with the unrelenting and insidious promotion of violence in film, on TV, through video games and in music have significantly enhanced the risk. Both motive and means for deadly violence have been ratcheted up to levels hard to imagine only a generation ago. In the chapters ahead I hope to make a compelling case for reducing private ownership of guns to levels more appropriate for our time.

The Second
Amendment Myth

Most of us have been convinced through the power of a frequently repeated myth, that the Constitution of the United States grants every citizen the right to keep and bear arms. This interpretation of the Second Amendment has been drilled into us so deeply that we accept it as an article of faith. But any serious examination of the Second Amendment—either in its original context or in the context of subsequent court decisions—clearly exposes this assumed article of faith as nothing more than the wishful thinking of gun advocates. The Second Amendment, in its entirety, states the following:

> "A well regulated militia, being necessary to the security of a free state, the right of the people to keep and bear arms, shall not be infringed."

Gun advocates focus on the second half of the amendment, which says "the right of the people to keep and bear arms, shall not be infringed." and conveniently ignore or gloss over the first half. The first half of the amendment explains that citizens were given the right to bear arms so they could participate in a "well-regulated militia", which is "necessary to the security of a free state." When the Constitution was written in the late 1700s, the colonist's battle for independence from Great Britain had only recently concluded. The fear of renewed hostilities with the defeated enemy or with other foreign powers that also had considerable interests in America ensured that a provision for raising armies would be included in the Constitution.

Now, more than 200 years later, it's difficult for us to comprehend how armies were raised in those days. Our notion of national defense is one of large standing armies, formed, supported and employed full time by the federal government. We have an Army, a Navy, an Air Force and a Marine Corps continually employed to protect the nation. Additional supplementary state units, known as the National Guard, are part-time members of the nation's armed forces, trained and available for deployment as needed. When the need for soldiers exceeds the existing troop strength, drafts have been implemented to acquire additional manpower. Our national defense structure has been configured and staffed in this way for more than a century.

Contrast our modern-day national defense structure with the way military protection was provided in our country's first century. Each state formed its own military unit, or militia. There was no federal prescription for organization, training and logistical support of state militias. Though operational practices varied considerably from state to state, all state militias had two features in common: 1) all able-bodied men were expected to make themselves available for service as needed, and 2) the weapons used by the militia were the personally owned firearms of the militiamen. This certainly would be a highly ineffective approach to national defense in our day; but circumstances were quite different then. It was not at all difficult to generate interest in serving in a state militia. Every state had sufficient need for protecting its borders and citizens, regardless of the national agenda. As the nation expanded from east to west, pioneers of newly forming states were constantly under attack from Native Americans and occasionally from French and Spanish settlers. Those on the front lines of advancing civilization were well armed. The firearms acquired for personal protection were the very same firearms that were used by armies throughout the world. Pioneering a new land was not for the faint of heart and the pioneers were always ready to defend self, family and property. Organizing together as militia to protect community and state was a very natural and necessary thing to do.

The state militia could be used to resolve localized conflicts or could be called to national service if necessary. It was more difficult to enlist state militias for a national cause, but not nearly as difficult as we might imagine it today. Patriotism was usually incentive enough to meet troop obligations. When it was inadequate, financial incentives, coercion and threat were employed. There were times when a state was unable to meet federal obligations, at which point the government would turn to a more willing or able state for support. It wasn't a perfect system, but the pioneering culture that prevailed through the western migration of the late 1800s ensured a steady stream of practiced and able-bodied gunmen to fill the ranks. In addition to state militias, the Constitution granted the federal government the power to establish standing professional military units of the Army and Navy, under the direction of the President of the United States as commander in chief. The full-time federal Army and Navy were organized soon after the United States government was formed but were never large enough to be sufficient for significant action. These initial national military organizations served more as a framework of leadership and direction to the state militias as those units were brought into national service.

The Civil War marked the point at which the state militia system began to break down. By that time the weapons of modern warfare had evolved far beyond the capabilities of the privately owned weapons in the hands of state militiamen. For example, the invention of the hand-cranked Gatling gun allowed a single gunman to fire nearly 3,000 rounds of ammunition a minute from one firearm. And it was soon replaced by true machine guns—lighter, faster and more devastating. At this juncture in history, the firearms used in warfare rapidly began to diverge in capability from firearms that were useful to civilians. These new weapons of war were either too expensive for individuals to afford, or in most cases, the firepower was far beyond any capability needed in civilian life. At exactly the same time, another trend was under way that also contributed to the demise of the militia system. The West was now nearly settled and the need for personal firearms was rapidly diminishing. The intersection of these two trends brought inevitable extinction to the state militia system by the early part of the 20th century. A modern remnant, the National Guard system, replaced the state militia; but it is very different in concept. National Guard units are organized, supported and staffed under the direction of the federal military. Unlike the state militia of old, the National Guard is not the primary component of our national defense. It provides experienced backup only in times of extreme need.

Because state militias as originally envisioned in the Constitution are no longer in existence, the Second Amendment is in essence null and void. It's an anachronism of an earlier age when private citizens and their personal firearms were the soldiers and arsenals of the nation. The amendment is written quite clearly. The right to bear arms was predicated on a need for militiamen. With that need gone, so too is the Constitutional right for citizens to keep and bear arms. This is a perfectly common sense conclusion for a layman to reach, and it's also a conclusion supported by several Supreme Court decisions. Gun advocates would have us believe otherwise; but the Court has clearly ruled on this issue, supporting this obvious conclusion. In 1939, the Supreme Court ruled in United States v. Miller that an individual's right to possess firearms is not protected by the Second Amendment unless ownership has "some reasonable relationship to the preservation or efficiency of a well-regulated militia." The Supreme Court has upheld that decision in several subsequent challenges, reiterating that the National Guard is the state militia of our time and Second Amendment protection applies only to firearms dedicated for use in the National Guard. In corollary decisions, the Supreme Court and several lower courts have also upheld very strict state gun control laws when those laws were challenged on the basis of violating the Second Amendment.

If both common sense and law are in agreement that the Constitution does not guarantee the right of a private citizen to keep and bear arms, why does the myth persist? I think it comes down to three factors—ignorance, tolerance and money. I use the word ignorance in its strictest sense and without desire to offend anyone. In fact, I put myself in this category. Prior to this effort I had never seriously read nor studied the Second Amendment and had assumed for most of my life that it granted the right to keep and bear arms to all citizens. Likewise, I had never before considered what the courts had determined concerning the Second Amendment and the efficacy of state firearm restrictions. I admit my ignorance was born of insufficient interest in the issue. I am certain that sometime during my high school and college education, and likely during yours as well, the Second Amendment was reviewed and discussed in reasonable depth. But at the time, I didn't have much interest in the topic and it all went in one ear and out the other. It seems that all I have heard about the Second Amendment in the intervening years has been that the right to bear arms is written in stone and supported by the courts. I am certain that gun control advocates have been attempting to enlighten us for years with the obvious fact that no such protection exists, but it somehow got lost on me. I suspect the same is true for many of us.

For those who already know that a Constitutional right to bear arms is a myth but nevertheless continue to support the right to bear arms, tolerance is the most likely motivation. I've been over this ground many times already in this book so I won't belabor the point. I will only briefly remind that there are many fellow citizens who personally don't own firearms and perhaps even believe it's dangerous for someone else to own them. Yet, they are reluctant to impose those views on gun owners. They have concluded that gun ownership is not a significant enough threat to the common good to call for a restriction on gun ownership. The sentiment of protecting another's rights is noble, but I believe in the case of private firearm ownership the negative effects on our society have been underestimated.

The final obstacle to debunking this myth is money. Those who have a lot of money can afford the biggest megaphones. In this case it's the gun lobby that can afford the big megaphone. The lobby is fueled by two special interest groups—seriously committed gun owners and gun manufacturers—who are willing to spend considerable sums of money and energy to perpetuate the myth. As I referenced earlier, only about 40 percent of us own guns, but that 40 percent is very serious about it. On average there are 4.4 guns per owner. Think about that. Common sense tells us that many gun owners only own one. To get up to an average of 4.4 guns per owner requires that a significant number of these gun owners have veritable arsenals in their homes. They are extremely committed and willing to expend money, time and energy to protect their right to continue to own firearms. There is also considerable passion on the other side of this issue; but I don't believe it's in the same league as the passion generated by firearm owners.

In fact, it would seem highly unlikely that another group could have a stronger passion for maintaining the free flow of firearms; but there is actually one group with even more passion and motivation for maintaining the status quo—gun manufacturers. You can well imagine the money and effort firearm manufacturers are willing and able to commit to ensure their products continue to fly off the shelves. It's a multi-billion dollar business with very good profit margins. The industry is certainly not bashful in its efforts to preserve its existence, but it can't give the appearance of being overly brash and motivated by self-interest either. That's why a third member of the "right-to-bear-arms trinity" serves as the primary mouthpiece for both gun manufacturers and owners—the National Rifle Association (NRA). The NRA is small but mighty. It only has approximately 4.3 million members, but its voice is amplified far beyond its natural means through coordinated lobbying efforts with gun manufacturers. It's hard to imagine a special interest group consisting of less than 1.5 percent of our population having such a significant influence, but pound for pound it's probably the most successful special interest lobby in Washington. The financial resources of the NRA are limited to member and donor contributions, but the gun manufacturers have very deep pockets. Such support ensures that the Second Amendment myth will not die easily.

If the Second Amendment is myth, what is it then that actually preserves the right to keep and bear arms? That right certainly exists. We see it all around us. Guns are everywhere. It has nothing to do with the Second Amendment—it's entirely a legislative matter. There are literally thousands of laws in place today that either preserve or restrict gun ownership. The vast majority of this legislation is in the form of local laws such as city ordinances that require licensing of handguns and other concealable weapons. With thousands of laws in place already, some wonder why gun control advocates continue to press for additional restrictions. The sad truth is that local laws are often ignored and ultimately unenforceable. With differing ordinances from city to city, it's nearly impossible to enforce these existing laws. Guns from more lenient states and cities flow freely into more restrictive areas without notice until something tragic happens. Gun control laws can only be effective if they are national in scope. Sadly, most federal firearm laws are focused on punishment and not prevention. Criminals who use firearms in the commission of a crime and persons who assist criminals in obtaining firearms are subject to severe mandatory federal punishment. But this deterrence seems to have little effect on the criminal distribution and use of firearms. Unfortunately, there are only a few federal gun control laws, such as the Brady Bill, that are preventative in nature—that actually seek to make it more difficult for criminals to acquire weapons in the first place. We have previously reviewed how mild the restrictions of the Brady Bill are, so it will come as no surprise that federal gun control laws are virtually impotent, and it will remain that way as long as we allow our elected officials to conveniently hide behind the myth of the Second Amendment as justification for rejecting gun control legislation. Don't be fooled by any Second Amendment excuse to justify inaction on gun control. It isn't about Constitutional rights, it's all about money. If campaign contributions from the NRA and gun manufacturers dried up, the Second Amendment myth would soon be exposed. With so much at stake for gun manufacturers, it won't happen that way. But the reverse is possible. If enough of us hold our representatives accountable for hiding behind a myth, real progress on gun control can be made. There is only one thing that a politician values more than campaign contributions—votes. The Second Amendment myth will cease to be a crutch for politicians only when it is clear that a majority of Americans see through the myth. I hope that day is soon.

The Protection Dilemma

Americans who own firearms acquire them primarily for three potential uses—hunting, hobby and protection. Hunting and hobby ownership are very similar in nature. Many hunters claim their motivation is to put food on the table, but in reality very few hunters make a necessary or even significant contribution to the household pantry. The fact of the matter is that gun use by both hunters and hobbyists is discretionary. If hunting and hobby firearms were not available, many would be deprived of the enjoyment those activities bring to their lives, but it wouldn't be a fatal or, in my opinion, even a significant deprivation. Life would go on, albeit minus one source of enjoyment and satisfaction. Other pastimes of a similar nature could and would be found to replace the gun hobby.

On the other hand, the motivation of those who acquire and use firearms for personal protection is very different. These gun owners aren't pursuing a hobby. They are concerned with protection of life and property. It's difficult to argue against the right of an individual to own a weapon to protect themselves and perhaps their family from criminal activity. We all share the fundamental desire to ensure that our lives, property and dignity are protected from anyone who would attempt to take them from us. After all, we live in a country founded on the principles of life, liberty and the pursuit of happiness. There is no liberty or happiness without life. Therefore, protection of life is the most fundamental right and responsibility granted to us.

Without a doubt, firearms wielded in self-defense by potential victims have averted crime and saved lives. But specifically how many crimes are averted and how many lives are saved by gun ownership? Given the nature of a criminal encounter and the variety of potential outcomes, it's very difficult to know. The only reliable statistics available are for lethal encounters where the criminal is actually shot dead by the victim. On average, between 300 and 500 criminals are killed in self-defense by potential victims each year. That isn't a large number in a country the size of ours, but we also know that for every criminal killed in self-defense many others are wounded or scared off. However, capturing reliable statistics for non-lethal self-defense is next to impossible. I've seen estimates ranging from less than 5,000 per year from anti-gun organizations to greater than 1 million per year from pro-gun organizations.

Putting aside specific numbers for now, it's undoubtedly true that a significant number of lives have been saved because a potential victim defended him or herself with a firearm. But there are several significant downsides to allowing every citizen to be equipped for a shootout with the bad guys. First and foremost is the likelihood that brandishing a weapon in self-defense might actually cause the criminal to initiate a shootout that might never have happened without the appearance of the victim's weapon. Surely most armed criminals would prefer that their weapon remains an unused threat in the successful completion of their crime. Discharging a firearm in the commission of a crime only enhances the risk and multiplies the punishment should the criminal be apprehended. It isn't possible to collect accurate statistics on the number of crimes committed with threatening weapons that are not discharged in the criminal act. But common sense alone would tell us that the majority of armed criminals are not very likely to use them if the crime proceeds as planned. There are more than 11 million crimes committed each year in the United States, including burglary, robbery, vehicle theft, rape and aggravated assault. Approximately 15,000 of those crimes are murders so we know the criminals in those cases were armed. But it's not possible to know how many of the criminals committing the remainder of the 11 million criminal acts a year have firearms in hand. Is it 10 percent? That would mean 1.1 million crimes are committed with a gun in hand but not used. Is it more than 10 percent? Is it less?

We will never know the exact number; however, from these statistics it seems certain to me that the number of times a firearm is actually used in the commission of a crime is miniscule when compared with the number of times a firearm is present but not used. In the same vein, isn't it likely that a considerable number of the 15,000 homicides committed each year are the result of a shootout between the criminal and the victim—a shootout that would not have occurred if the victim had not attempted to use a weapon in self-defense? Once weapons are drawn, who do you think most often is equipped with better fire power and more developed firearm skills, the victim or the criminal? There is no doubt in my mind that in the vast majority of criminal encounters, the criminal will have better weapons and be more skilled in using them. Unless the victim catches the criminal entirely by surprise, it's not likely to be a fair fight. In a gunfight between an amateur and a professional, who would you bet on? How many victims saved by firearm protection are counterbalanced by victims lost in shootouts that never would have occurred without the appearance of the victim's weapon?

In addition to the likelihood that the criminal will out-shoot the intended victim, once gunfire erupts, many other truly bad things can happen. Even the best trained gunmen make mistakes in the heat of battle. How many times have we heard accounts of policemen shooting themselves, other officers or even innocent by-standers in the confusion of a shootout? It happens all too frequently with the pros. Imagine what happens when less-skilled weapon handlers pull the trigger. Surely many gun owners each year wound, kill or maim themselves and other innocents in the course of defending themselves with a weapon. How many lives saved in defensive shootouts are thus offset by innocent victims of stray gunfire from a shootout triggered by the appearance of a defensive weapon?

Besides the likely skill differential between criminal and victim, the criminal also has a substantial logistical advantage. Crime is not a scheduled activity that allows the victim time to plan and prepare a defense. Weapons must be easily accessible to provide protection on the spur of the moment. The need for accessibility pretty much rules out the use of rifles and other large firearms for self-defense. Rarely is there time during the commission of a crime for the victim to retrieve a rifle from the gun closet. That makes the logical weapon of choice for personal protection the concealable handgun, which can be carried on the body, in a purse, in the glove box or anywhere else close enough to be useful if necessary. But merely having the gun nearby is not enough to provide adequate protection. The firearm must also be loaded and ready to fire. Literally millions of Americans are armed with loaded handguns, ready to fire for their own protection. Consider the risks introduced by this system of self-protection. If you have ever used a handgun, you know very well how difficult it is to shoot one accurately. Proficiency with a handgun requires considerable skill that can only be developed through long hours of practice. But when handguns are purchased, no testing of basic handgun skills occurs and no training is required. Many handgun owners invest the time to develop and maintain appropriate skills but most don't. We all probably know someone who has purchased a handgun for protection and only fired it in practice a minimal number of times. Handguns drawn by inexperienced owners represent a great risk to the innocent. A poorly aimed handgun is as likely to injure or kill the defender or innocent bystanders as it is to stop the criminal.

It's also conceivable, and in fact it happens quite frequently, that a crime victim in the excitement of the moment fires on a criminal without even knowing if the criminal is armed. The reason for this is simple logic: If you don't get off the first shot in a shootout, you might not get off any shots at all. If the criminal fires first, chances are good that the victim won't even have a chance to use his weapon in self-defense. So the victim must pull the trigger with only the scantiest of information at hand. There isn't time to sort it all out. It doesn't happen often, but we have all heard of cases when unarmed criminals were killed by armed victims. Guess what happens to the self-defense argument in that case? Criminal becomes victim and victim becomes criminal. It's a costly role reversal for the intended victim.

Even if the victim successfully thwarts a crime by using a weapon, how often do you think the victim will face the same experience again? It has to be a very rare occurrence that any single person is victimized more than once by an armed criminal. That means any handgun purchased for self-protection is idle during 99 percent of its lifetime. As I've stated before, to be useful, a handgun must always be loaded and readily accessible. But if the gun is loaded and accessible to the owner, it is also loaded and accessible to many others. The weapon can easily end up in the hands of an inexperienced user, maybe even a child, who can inadvertently do great harm to themselves or others. We've all heard accounts of the great tragedies that occur when children find and play with loaded weapons. Such incidents don't represent a large number of deaths and injuries, but there are enough such disasters to offset some of the lives saved by defensive weapons. A more likely possibility is that the easily accessible weapon ends up in the hands of someone with evil intent. Criminals who might be stymied by a background check while purchasing a gun often avoid the hassle and save some money by stealing firearms from private owners instead. In essence, between the infrequent opportunities for usage, the defensive handgun is an accident waiting to happen. And the accident is often fatal.

Throughout this discussion I have attempted to indicate that though some lives are saved because potential victims are armed for self-protection, other lives are needlessly lost as the act of self-protection itself initiates events that can have unintended and even lethal consequences for criminal targets and innocent by-standers alike. It's impossible to accurately determine which side of the balance scale—life saved or life lost—has greater weight. Since it's impossible to collect accurate data, both sides, pro-gun and pro-gun control, claim victory in this debate. Who are we to believe? My own common sense and experience tells me that it's probably close to a wash at best.

That seems to coincide with the experience expressed in the Gallup Poll that I referenced in a previous chapter:

Gun Ownership:

- Percentage of all adult Americans owning a gun   40%

    Does Having a Gun in the House Make You Safer:

- Yes   42%

- No, more dangerous   46%

    —Gallup Poll, January 4th, 2005

Forty-six percent of respondents believe that guns owned for protection are likely to be more dangerous than helpful. I agree.

But even if I was convinced that the balance was heavily weighted in favor of guns being an effective protection from crime, I would still argue against their use for that purpose. Why? For me, the most commonly asked questions—how many crimes are prevented and how many lives are saved by privately owned firearms—aren't even the right questions to ask. The question we ought to be asking is this: Is allowing an entire population to acquire firearms for self-protection the way a civilized nation in this day and age ought to provide for the safety and protection of its citizens? To me the answer is clear. If safety and protection are the objectives, there has got to be a better way than "every man for himself." The Gallup poll mentioned above indicates there is widespread support for that sentiment as well. It might not be obvious from the polling data, but through simple math it's an obvious conclusion to reach. Only 40 percent of Americans own firearms. That means 60 percent have decided that owning a firearm for protection is either not necessary or is too dangerous. Therefore a reasonable majority of us is already convinced that guns are not a responsible and reasonable form of self-protection. Only our reluctance to restrict the rights of a 40 percent minority keeps us from implementing gun control laws that would stop some of the violence and damage generated by the arsenal of weapons theoretically deployed for self-defense.

Individuals who arm themselves for personal protection are in essence assuming a role that ought to be provided by professionals. The safety and protection of citizens is one of the primary reasons for the existence of government. If violent crimes are occurring at an intolerable level, putting guns in the hands of private citizens is a case of treating the symptoms and not curing the disease. If ownership of individual firearms was the system of choice for self-protection all of us would need to be armed. But we know from our own experience that arming ourselves is not necessary. Otherwise, how do the 60 percent of us who are not armed survive? We have heard many times that a multitude of crimes are stopped before they ever start because criminals are afraid that their victims will be armed. Pro-gun advocates are quick to conclude that if guns are not available for self-defense, criminals will have less fear and, therefore, armed crime will actually increase. It's just not true. Right now a criminal has a better than a 60 percent chance of confronting an unarmed victim by choosing someone at random. However, most criminals are far from random, choosing weak and obvious targets over armed and difficult ones. It would seem more logical to assume that if criminals fear armed victims, then currently crime is at least partially being redirected to the unarmed among us. Personally, I have my doubts about that. I don't think armed victims are a significant concern for serious, practiced criminals. Would a professional killer be overly fearful of an amateur handgun owner? But for the sake of argument, let's assume it's true. Then the 60 percent who are unarmed and feel well enough protected without personal firearms ought to request that the 40 percent who are armed give up their weapons and enter the potential victim pool. It would spread the risk of crime on any given individual considerably.

I fully recognize the dilemma we face in considering whether or not individuals ought to be allowed firearms for personal protection. Certainly some lives are saved and many crimes averted every year because of firearms wielded successfully by potential victims of crime. And it is likely that a substantial portion of the 40 percent of Americans who own firearms believe their weapons are necessary for personal protection. But there is a better way. The solution is to fix the systems that protect us from crime instead of "going around them" by arming individuals to fight their own battles. The every-man-for-himself mentality might have been the right solution in the days of the Wild West, but it is not the right solution for today.

Guns Don't Kill

It's certainly safe to say that nearly every adult in America has heard of the National Rifle Association. This well-known and influential organization is dedicated to preventing the enactment of any legislation that would restrict private ownership of firearms and for the past 125 years the NRA has done a very good job of accomplishing this objective. In a previous chapter, I pointed out how difficult it has been to pass even minor restrictions on firearms. You might recall that after the failed attempt to assassinate President Reagan it took an entire decade of considerable effort to facilitate the enactment of the Brady Bill. And for all of that effort, the only restriction imposed by this bill is a database check to ensure that handgun dealers do not sell handguns to known criminals. You might also recall that there have been absolutely no additional restrictions implemented in response to the Columbine High School massacre. Why is it so difficult to enact any form of gun control legislation? The answer can be expressed in three letters—NRA. The National Rifle Association is the source of this powerful resistance, and by any measure, its influence and effectiveness are extraordinary.

How does an organization with only 4 million members wield such disproportionate influence? With the same assets that are used by all successful capitalist enterprises—sufficient funding and brilliant marketing. Only a small portion of the funding for the battle against gun control comes directly from the NRA and its membership. Most of the funding is provided by gun manufacturers who have an obvious vested interest in preserving everyone's right to purchase firearms.

Though gun manufacturers spend vast sums of money on campaign contributions, political action committees and pro-gun advertisements, it's done subtly, behind the scenes, while the NRA—an organization that in theory represents sincere, concerned citizens—is the public face in the battle against gun control. The reason for this arrangement is obvious. Americans are by nature extremely skeptical of self-serving crusades led by big-business; so having the NRA at the forefront of the anti-gun control crusade is much more effective than a cause led by a massive industry whose billions of dollars in profits are dependent on the outcome.

In addition to the substantial financial resources at its disposal, the National Rifle Association is a very clever and effective public relations machine. The NRA has two stated missions. The first is to ensure that everyone has unrestricted access to guns. The second is to serve the interests of gun owners by providing education, training and support programs. I recently visited the NRA's Web site and was reminded of this dual mission by the following slogans that were prominently displayed:

- "NRA. Protecting your Second Amendment freedom"

- "NRA—Offering America's preeminent shooting, training, educational and public service programs that foster the safe, responsible ownership and use of firearms."

The second slogan is repeated over and over again in a continuous loop as a slide show of endorsements flashes on your computer screen. Endorsers at this time include actor Charlton Heston, former president of the NRA; athletes Nolan Ryan and Karl Malone; former U.S. Rep. JC Watts; country music great Charlie Daniels; and finally, Wayne Lapierre, chief executive officer of the NRA. This is obviously a very small sample of the total number of celebrities who support the National Rifle Association. Over the years, we have all become familiar with the large number of highly visible personalities who support the NRA. If the Web site is not updated frequently with other celebrity endorsements it certainly could be.

This dual mission of the National Rifle Association makes perfect sense. The association exists to ensure all Americans have the right to purchase firearms and once purchased, to assist us in using them safely and professionally. The two missions are not only logical, but they also appeal to basic American values—protecting individual rights and enhancing our personal safety. What's there to argue with? On the surface it all sounds great. But below the surface, to me, it is nothing more than an incredibly effective "spin" machine. Focusing attention on gun safety is nothing more than a clever method of diverting attention from the NRA's primary objective—the preservation of profits made by the manufacturers of firearms. Of course leaders of the NRA would never describe their primary mission in that way. They prefer to package it as "protecting our Second Amendment freedom," which is a misleading statement. As I've discussed earlier, it is nothing more than a myth that the Second Amendment grants us the right to keep and bear arms. The leaders of the NRA certainly know this, but are also smart enough to know that pretending to protect your constitutional rights is a more attractive proposition than stating the truth, which would have to be something along the lines of "lobbying the Congress of the United States to ensure that additional gun control laws are not passed."

Any right we have to keep and bear arms comes from legislation, not the Constitution. There is a significant difference between rights protected by the Constitution and rights granted by a legislative body. Constitutional rights are almost immutable. Such rights can only be lost through the process of amending the Constitution, which is a difficult and time consuming process. It can't happen unless there is overwhelming public support for an amendment. A simple mathematical majority is not adequate. An overwhelming two-thirds majority is required to amend the Constitution. On the other hand, laws instituted by a legislature aren't nearly as difficult to overturn or modify, nor do they have the same level of respect as a Constitutional right. We expect some level of permanence from what was written by our Founding Fathers, but we don't expect permanence from a legislature composed of competing political parties. We have become accustomed to the reversal of legislation when the leadership of a legislature is overturned in an election. We all recognize that current laws are a reflection of current politics and have the permanence of the current weather. Thus the National Rifle Association's deceptive spin of this issue is very effective. By pretending to protect Constitutional rights that don't really exist they avoid admitting they are actually working to preserve laws that could easily be overturned or modified.

The NRA public relations spin doesn't stop there. The organization has very wisely and effectively instituted training programs and public service campaigns in support of responsible gun ownership. Through this effort, the NRA has provided a very useful and important service to America and should be commended for it. I have no doubt that safety has been enhanced and lives saved as a result of such NRA programs. I don't want to minimize their contribution, but unfortunately it's a positive contribution that the National Rifle Association cleverly uses as a focal point to divert attention away from its primary mission of preserving unrestricted access to firearms.

It's a fantastic public relations strategy. An organization involved in such an obviously good thing can't possibly be bad, can it? And I repeat again, the NRA is to be commended for the good resulting from this second mission. But this good comes at the expense of the great harm caused by the proliferation of personal weapons. And who really believes that safety is the primary concern of the National Rifle Association? It's a secondary concern, necessary for the public image of the NRA, but not sufficient in and of itself for its existence. If a new organization was spun off from the National Rifle Association, leaving the NRA to focus on the Second Amendment while the new organization focused on safety, would the NRA continue to be as powerful and effective as it is today? I think not. There must be many who appreciate the NRA's safety programs but are turning a blind eye to its other objectives. The NRA spin of promoting firearm safety while at the same time promoting firearm proliferation is the equivalent of Smokey the Bear teaching us to prevent forest fires while at the same time promoting the proliferation of matches. It wouldn't work for Smokey, but it certainly has been effective for the National Rifle Association.

The NRA spin is usually very effective but it has been surprisingly inept in some of its efforts to influence public opinion. When Charlton Heston was president of the National Rifle Association, he addressed crowds of NRA members on several occasions with the now infamous act of holding a rifle in his hand, lifting it high over his head and declaring that anyone attempting to take away his right to bear arms would have to take the rifle "from his cold, dead hand." The performance was reminiscent of Heston's famous portrayal of Moses in the film "The Ten Commandments," where Moses dramatically lifts the sacred stone tablets over his head for all to see. It was quite a dramatic sight to see this former "Moses" holding a rifle in place of the stone tablets and, not surprisingly, it was well received by the NRA faithful. For most others, it was an example of over-the-top hyperbole, and Heston's standing in the public eye suffered considerably. And rightly so. It was an ill-informed and shallow performance. It might have rallied the faithful, but it likely diminished the National Rifle Association in the eyes of the general public.

As ridiculous as Heston's defiant declaration was, my favorite ridiculous statement from the National Rifle Association is the often-repeated phrase, "guns don't kill people, people do." The phrase has been so widely used in defense of firearm ownership that I would be greatly surprised if you haven't heard it many times yourself. On the surface it's a clever play on words. It's easy to remember, and the sentiment might at first ring true. After all, a person does have to pull the trigger to kill with a firearm, and we put people, not firearms, in jail when murders are committed. But the sole purpose of this statement is to divert attention away from the weapon involved in the killing. It's the equivalent of saying that "airplanes don't fly, people do." We all know that people can't fly, but an airplane makes it possible. Likewise, people don't shoot other people without a weapon. It takes a firearm to make it possible. The person and the weapon are inextricably linked. Neither one on its own is sufficient for completion of the act. The National Rifle Association's effort to focus solely on the person is nothing more than the public relations equivalent of the classic shell game. The NRA hopes we will keep focused on the shell that represents the killer while they continue to protect the shell that represents the weapon that made the killing possible.

Shell games might be clever politics, but the use of this strategy is at best shallow, and at worst, dishonest. It's indisputable that firearms facilitate the deaths of approximately 25,000 Americans every year. If there were no guns, it's likely that nearly all of those deaths would be avoided. Sure, the motive for murder would be strong enough in some cases that another weapon would be found and used. Knives, baseball bats, poison, and a host of other weapons could and would be used to commit murders. But common sense tells us that none of these potential weapons provides the ease, overwhelming power and finality of a gun. With a gun available, all it takes is ready, aim, fire. That's it. It's not honest to say that a significant number of these firearm deaths would occur anyway with another weapon. Is there any doubt that sensible gun restrictions would save many from being added to the death roll each year? Guns in isolation don't kill people, but guns in the hands of people sure do. It "takes two to tango," and that deadly tango happens altogether too often. Remove the firearm owner from the deadly encounter and a death is avoided. And the corollary is also true. Remove the firearm from the owner and a death is avoided.

Returning to the question that opened this chapter, why is it so difficult to pass even the most minor restrictions on firearms? The National Rifle Association has ferociously resisted any legislation that would restrict firearms, and by any measure it has been remarkably successful in that mission. But any advocacy organization that spends more time deflecting attention away from the very object it advocates must not have a good product to sell. I hope a significant number of Americans recognize the self-serving motivation of the National Rifle Association and see through the publicity spin it uses to great effect in short circuiting any attempt to legislate firearm restrictions.

Curbing a Violent Culture

Gun control advocates seem to spend an inordinate amount of energy focusing on accidental firearm deaths as a primary reason to implement gun control legislation. They often share tragic stories of children who find loaded weapons and accidentally shoot themselves or others. But the number of fatalities from the accidental discharge of firearms is actually quite small. In fact, the number of accidental deaths by firearms each year is significantly lower than the number of deaths caused by other types of accidents for which we readily accept the mortality rate. Motor vehicle accidents, fires, drowning and suffocation all kill more people each year than firearm accidents. Preventing accidental deaths is certainly a worthy goal and ought to be vigorously pursued. Passing legislation that requires firearm safety devices—like trigger locks—can save a number of lives each year. But the vast majority of lives lost at gunpoint are not lost accidentally. Firearm fatalities are almost always an intentional outcome not an accident. We should certainly continue to pursue safety devices that will reduce the number of accidental firearm deaths, but to make a significant reduction in the number of deaths caused by firearms we need to focus more time and energy on the intentional use of firearms.

To establish the magnitude of the problem in the United States, consider the following annual statistics:

- 11,829 firearm homicides

- 17,108 firearm suicides

- Gunshot wounds are the leading cause of death for young men, even exceeding motor vehicle accidents and the total of all disease related deaths. Ten young people (under age 20) are killed each day.

  —Deaths: Final Data for 2002, National Center for Health
  Statistics

Unfortunately, the 28,937 firearm deaths in 2002 are not an aberration. Statistics from prior years indicate that on average 25,000 firearm deaths per year would be a conservative estimate. In addition to the more than 25,000 who die at gunpoint each year, there are obviously a large number who are only wounded. It's estimated that as many as 75,000 to 90,000 are wounded each year. In a nation of nearly 300 million people, 25,000 dead and 75,000 wounded each year might seem to be a relatively minor concern. But it's not. These statistics indicate that each and every day approximately 70 people die from intentional firearm usage, and another 200 people are wounded. That's every day. Imagine what the toll would be during a typical human lifetime. If we assume that an average human lifetime is 75 years and that the firearm death rate continues at the current level, the number of fellow citizens that will be lost during a typical lifetime will exceed 1.8 million. Nearly 5.5 million more will be wounded. To put this in perspective, consider how this projected number of firearm deaths at home in America compares to the number of casualties America has experienced in foreign wars during the past half century:

Conflict	Dead	Duration in Years	Avg. Deaths Per Year
Word War II	295,000	2.5	118,00
Korea	54,000	3	18,000
Vietnam	58,000	11	5,300

| Iraq (as of Nov. 14, 2005) | 2,068 | 2.67 | 775 |
| Living in the United States | 1,800,000 | 75 | 25,000 |

It's shocking that only World War II had a higher annual death rate than the death rate we experience year after year right here in our own country, where we are theoretically at peace. Looking at the statistics from another angle, we will lose more people to gunfire here in the United States every 17 years than we lost in all four of these wars combined. Americans have a very strong aversion to war. None of us wants to have a brother, sister, mother or father end up dead in a foreign war zone. Our aversion to war is so strong that we protest any possibility of war and build monuments to the deceased when war cannot be avoided. Yet within the borders of our own land, we tolerate loss of life that exceeds levels experienced on gruesome battle fields far from home. And in response, there is only meager and insufficient protest. The only monuments dedicated to the victims of homeland gunfire are the lonely and often inconspicuous headstones in local cemeteries.

It's also enlightening to examine where the United States stands relative to the rest of the world in gun-related deaths. Based on what I have already said, it's probably not surprising that of the 36 wealthiest countries in the world, we are very near the top of the list. Here are some representative examples:

Gun-Related Deaths per 100,000 Population

- Brazil   12.95
- Mexico   12.69
- United States   10.50
- Northern Ireland   6.63
- Finland   6.46
- Switzerland   5.31

- France   5.15
- Canada   4.31
- Israel   2.91
- Italy   2.44
- Germany   1.24
- England and Wales   0.41
- Japan   0.05

—International Journal of Epidemiology 1998:27:216 for foreign statistics
—Deaths: Final Data for 2002, National Center for Health Statistics for US statistics

Though I expected we would be at or near the top of this list, the magnitude of the difference between us and the rest of the world is shocking. If we set aside Brazil and Mexico—both well known for lawlessness and violence—an American is more than two times more likely to be shot than a Frenchman, 4 times more than an Italian, 8 times more than a German and 25 times more than a Briton. I won't even attempt to calculate the enormous difference between the United States and Japan. It's truly an eye-opening and discouraging picture.

Why is there such an embarrassingly extreme level of gun violence in the United States? The roots of this homeland violence are long and deep. The pioneers who settled this land had to be familiar with weapons and skilful in their use. We aren't long removed from a generation of armed pioneers who sometimes shot their way across the western part of the United States. Unfortunately we are still close enough in time to this heritage that it remains in our cultural DNA. When the victims of westward expansion were completely subdued, it would have seemed likely that a maturing nation would rapidly discard its firearms and settle into a more peaceful and less violent culture. It's to be expected that this move away from violence wouldn't happen over night as any cultural change takes time. But surely within the advance of an entire century such change should have been made.

Yet the desire to own and use firearms has never been higher in our entire history, though there has not been a true need for them for a long time. Why are firearms so desired when they really have no practical use? To find a significant part of the answer to that question, all you have to do is turn on a television, listen to the radio, go to a movie or watch your children play video games. In the old days—days that many of us can clearly remember—American culture was developed and handed down from one generation to another around the family dinner table, in the family room, at the community hall and from uplifting books, television shows and movies. Today cultural development is more likely facilitated by a digital stream of information and images coming at us in variety of forms, uninterrupted, 24 hours of every day. And the digital pipeline that delivers this flow of information is insatiable. Vast quantities of digital content have to be produced to fill this ever expanding pipeline that never shuts down. There is always more demand in the pipeline than there is supply of content to feed it. Thus almost any digital content that's produced finds its way into the pipeline. Unfortunately for America, far too much of this content is flat-out violent. And in it, firearm violence is particularly featured and in many cases glorified.

The producers and distributors of this "entertainment" are quick to claim that there is no proven link between watching violence and acting violent. In this they are clearly wrong. The human mind is like a sponge soaking up everything it comes in contact with. Anything that enters can leave a permanent trail whether we want it to or not. While this can't be proven in a court of law, it certainly can be proven in the court of common sense. It's an act of extreme rationalization to insist that watching violence does not breed violence. We rationalize that it's alright because we are either too lazy to censor it, too hooked to stop it, or too timid to impose our personal distaste for violence on others. Our society pays a deadly price for this rationalization in terms of violent acts committed. But violence is not the only damaging outcome. Even those who never commit violent acts pay a steep personal price. It can't be good to have these violent images floating around inside our minds all of the time. It's a total waste of mental capacity and energy to have a portion of our minds processing such things while another portion is likely working overtime to suppress them.

It's interesting that the technologies necessary to provide this digital capability arrived at about the same time that the true need for privately owned firearms was rapidly declining. Not only has this proliferation of violent entertainment prolonged our country's fascination with personal firearms, but it has also magnified our interest as if through a telescopic lens. In previous times, a person was very infrequently exposed to firearm violence. Though gun violence existed, most people managed to go their entire lives without ever witnessing it up close and personal. Now we have the opportunity to witness multiple episodes of gun violence every day of our lives. That's some progress.

Unfortunately, this culture of violence is likely to continue unabated. It will not be curbed easily, if at all. Turning the tide would likely require restrictions that will be viewed by many as censorship of speech and ideas. We all know what a battle that would be. Perhaps some small progress will be made in curbing demand for violent programming, improving parental access controls and so on, but such things are a topic for another time. My point here is that powerful sources promoting gun violence exist and will continue to exist. We don't have an effective way to curb this problem any time soon. We need to face the reality that the genie is out of the bottle, and putting it back, if that is even possible, will take a long time. Of course we can make some inroads and should do everything in our power to curb the flow of violence. But even if the sources were shut down completely, effective today, there are hundreds of millions of us who are already programmed from the exposure to violence we have already experienced. It would be an entire generation before a significant lessening of cultural violence was completely in effect. Unfortunately, it just isn't possible in the short term to have a major impact on firearm violence by changing the personality of the firearm owner. The only way to have a serious impact on firearm violence is to limit the availability of firearms. Restricting gun ownership would not offer complete relief from this creeping devastation either. Homicides would still be committed by criminals with illegal firearms or other deadly weapons. Suicides would still be administered through other means. But how can we not believe that the violence would be reduced considerably? A rational person would come to the conclusion that a very significant number of wrongful deaths could be prevented by getting rid of some of the firepower that is all around us.

In response, the National Rifle Association and others will of course resist with everything in their power, including another well-worn slogan, "If guns are outlawed, only outlaws will have guns." Let's not be fooled by another diversion from the NRA. They prefer to shift the focus to the outlaws, not the guns. It's certain that outlaws will have a harder time getting guns with fewer in circulation. But I readily admit that even with stronger restrictions in place, outlaws will have guns just as they do now, and they will continue to commit crimes. But the level at which crime will occur is entirely dependent on the level of law enforcement opposing it, not by the number of firearms in private hands. As I've pointed out in a previous chapter, the best way to deter armed criminals is increasing the level of law enforcement applied against crime, not arming every citizen for self-defense. With 60 percent of us unarmed now, outlaws have an almost limitless pool of unarmed victims to prey on already.

For further confirmation that reducing the number of legally owned firearms will not lead to an increase in homicides, we need only to look at the results in other countries which have already applied strict controls on the acquisition of personal firearms. Contrary to the National Rifle Association's fear mongering, the safest countries in the world, relative to homicides committed, are countries with strict gun controls. Consider three major European countries—the United Kingdom, France and Germany. Gun control laws in all three are nearly identical. In essence, hunting guns are allowed for nearly everyone and can be obtained with minimal restriction. But acquiring a firearm for anything but hunting is quite difficult. An applicant is required to demonstrate a true need for personal protection and is then scrutinized by law enforcement officials to ensure not only the need, but also the reliability of the potential firearm owner. With these restrictions in place, many homes have firearms appropriate for sporting activities, but very few have handguns or other types of firearms. According to the National Rifle Association, we should expect a significant increase in homicides committed in these countries on unarmed victims who have no weapons to defend themselves. Following the logic of the NRA, these countries have outlawed guns and now only the outlaws have guns. So how do these societies fare in relation to the United States?

Firearm Homicides per 100,000 Population

- France   .4
- Germany   .2
- England and Wales   .08
- United States   4.1

—International Journal of Epidemiology 1998:27:216 for foreign statistics
—Deaths: Final Data for 2002, National Center for Health Statistics for US statistics

Here in the United States, where both outlaws and potential victims are armed, the homicide rate is ten times the rate in France, 20 times the rate in Germany and 50 times the rate in England and Wales. And these are not isolated examples. Similar results can be found for any country with more restrictive gun control laws than we have in the United States. The NRA slogan is clever and appealing on the surface, but is 180 degrees from reality.

So what can be done to curb the violence in our culture? I certainly agree that we ought to work to minimize or eliminate the underlying cultural influences that motivate people to use firearms in dangerous and deadly ways. But curbing this culture of violence is a long-term project. In the meantime, we can save many lives by restricting firearm ownership. I am not suggesting banning all privately owned firearms. I started this subject with an observation that there are three reasons for private ownership of guns—hunting, hobby and protection. Hunting with rifles and shotguns is such an inbred and established part of our heritage that I think we ought to leave it pretty much intact. The only change I would suggest is that we do something to ensure that weapons purchased for hunting are appropriate to the task. They should be equipped with enough fire power to ensure hunting is a sport and not a slaughter. No hunter should need a machine gun to kill an unarmed deer or a guided missile to bring down a duck. As for protection, let's apply the European model, making it possible to obtain a firearm for individual protection, but not until law enforcement officials agree that the weapon is necessary, the owner is responsibly trained in its use and will be reliable in its safe keeping. Finally, for those who collect and shoot firearms as a hobby, and the firearms collected are inappropriate for hunting purposes, I would say, sorry you're out of luck. Take up another hobby. I'm sure there are many responsible hobbyists who derive great pleasure from owning and shooting guns, but there are plenty of other hobbies that can offer similar enjoyment and benefits. It's not a significant sacrifice to make for the good of society, and we should not be timid in requiring it.

Separation of Church and State

The Culture War is a relatively new phenomenon. Three of the four issues that define the Culture War are products of the last 40 years or so. But the fourth issue—the debate over the role of religion in American government—has been around for a very long time. In fact, the debate over the appropriate degree of separation of church and state commenced well before the day the Constitution of the United States was ratified on June 21, 1788, and the debate has continued for the entire 217 years since ratification. Over the course of more than two centuries, the degree of separation between church and state has shifted slowly and marginally from one side to the other, like a pendulum moving at glacial speed. In our country's formative years, the pendulum was certainly moving in the direction of less separation. During our lifetime the pendulum has most certainly been moving in the direction of increased separation. Two events that occurred during the build-up to the 2004 presidential election illustrate the framework of the current debate, and the heat this issue continues to generate in spite of its advanced age.

The first event played out in the blue state of Alabama, reaching a legal, but certainly not a political, conclusion on Nov. 11, 2003. Alabama Chief Justice Roy Moore was removed from office for refusing to obey a federal court order to remove a monument engraved with the Ten Commandments from the public rotunda of the Alabama state courthouse. Justice Moore had blatantly engineered the confrontation with the American Civil Liberties Union. First, he refused any moderation in his public display of a monument clearly associated with Christianity. And second, he defied the order of the federal court that the monument be removed on constitutional grounds. The State of Alabama, Court of the Judiciary, unanimously agreed that Moore could not defy the law and continue to serve as a judge. He could no longer hold others accountable for obeying the law when he was in violation of the law himself. Justice Moore stood steadfast in his fight against the very legal system he represented, saying, the day the ruling was handed down, "I have absolutely no regrets. I have done what I was sworn to do. It's about whether or not you can acknowledge God as the source of our law and our liberty. That's all I've done. I've been found guilty."

As you would expect, Roy Moore was a hero to many red voters who believe that the very foundation of government is experiencing clearly damaging erosion by the slow but constant wear of anti-religious force. On the other hand, blue voters saw Justice Moore as a vanquished bigot, another self-righteous, intolerant Christian using the power of government to advocate his personal religious beliefs. Through legal appeals and unending self-promotion, both sides continued to annoy each other and inflame the debate during the entire presidential election process.

The second event played out in the blue state of California in the form of a legal challenge to the wording of the Pledge of Allegiance:

> "I pledge allegiance to the flag of the United States of America, and to the republic for which it stands, **one nation under God**, indivisible, with liberty and justice for all."

Michael Newdow, an avowed atheist from Sacramento, California, filed a lawsuit on behalf of his elementary school daughter to strike the language "one nation under God" from the Pledge of Allegiance. The school district, which is clearly an instrument of state government, required the children to recite the Pledge every day, just as many school districts around the country do. In Newdow's view, the phrase is an endorsement of God—an endorsement that any government entity, including schools, is forbidden from making by the Constitution. The 9th U. S. Circuit Court of Appeals agreed with him.

As expected, this ruling generated a furious backlash. The furor was exacerbated by the fact that the 9th U. S. Circuit Court of Appeals is located in the San Francisco Bay area, the epicenter of progressive liberalism, and this court has a longstanding reputation for liberal rulings that are often subsequently overturned on appeal. Public opinion polls indicated that a vast majority of Americans were outraged with Newdow and the 9th Circuit Court, including many who ordinarily support measures that ensure separation of church and state. To nearly everyone, this was a case of unnecessary nit-picking. The statement, "one nation under God" in the Pledge of Allegiance has no reference to any specific religion, making it adaptable or acceptable to most any person with a belief in any form of God. It would seem atheists are the only group who could interpret it as anti-constitutional, not in the sense that it promotes a specific religion, but that it promotes religion in general.

This battle was lopsided from the start. Even most Democrats, who are avowedly more in favor of separation of church and state than most Republicans, were against the decision. They were probably greatly disappointed that it was ever filed. It provided Republicans with a tremendous opening in an election year to paint the Democrats as both frivolous in their pursuit to remove God from government and anti-patriotic in attempting to attack the Pledge of Allegiance during a time of war. The Republicans were able to capitalize to great effect, and I am sure the whole episode cost the Democrats many votes in the November election of 2004.

Given the nature of the dispute and the heat of the issue in an election year, it was inevitable that this conflict would end up in the Supreme Court. Appropriately, on Flag Day, June 14, 2004, the Supreme Court overturned the ruling on a technicality. It turned out that Mr. Newdow was not legally the child's guardian and therefore had no legal right to speak for her. Thus the suit was invalid from the start. It was a welcome solution for the Supreme Court. It avoided the political drama that likely would have unfolded with a ruling on the merits of the case. Chief Justice William Rehnquist agreed with the solution, but also took the opportunity to write a separate opinion in which he stated the Pledge of Allegiance recited by school children as currently written does not violate the Constitution. Justice Sandra Day O'Conner and Justice Clarence Thomas also signed his opinion, giving us an interesting insight into how three of the Justices would have ruled on the case had it been necessary.

These two incidents are a good representation of the fundamental issues that have been debated for so long. We all certainly recall from our earliest education that separation of church and state is a fundamental principle incorporated into our Constitution by the Founding Fathers. But, on the other hand we are taught that the Founding Fathers were deeply religious, and their religion infused, if not inspired, nearly every principle of the government they worked to establish. It's certainly true that many of the Founding Fathers were deeply religious, as was most of the nation at the time. To this day we continue to be a very religious nation. A recent poll of religious affiliation and strength recorded the following:

How important would you say religion is in your own life?

Very Important	Fairly Important	Not Very Important	No Opinion
59%	24%	16%	1%

How often do you attend church or synagogue?

Once a Week	Almost Every Week	Once a Month	Seldom or Never
34%	10%	15%	41%

What is your religious affiliation, if any?

Protestant	Catholic	Other Christian	Other, Non-Christian	No Religion	No Response
50%	24%	10%	5%	9%	2%

—Gallup Poll, December 23, 2004

An interesting portrait of the influence of religion on politics is evident in this poll. To summarize the findings relevant to the topic at hand:

• Nearly 85 percent of Americans say religion is very important or fairly important in their own life

• Nearly 85 percent identify themselves with some form of Christianity

• A small minority of 10 percent have no religious affiliation

• Though nearly 90 percent identify with some form of religion, only 40 percent attend church on a regular basis

We have all been instructed in enough American history to understand that many of the early settlers of this country came here to escape religious persecution in Europe. It's certainly true that Pilgrim and Puritan roots are deep in New England. But after the initial waves of immigration to America, not all who came to the New World were motivated by a quest for religious freedom. By the time of the massive immigration of the late 1800s and early 1900s, religious intolerance was no longer a significant issue throughout most of Europe. Immigrants were attracted to America for other reasons, which were as varied as the immigrants themselves—jobs, opportunity and upward mobility most likely topped the list. I'm fairly certain that it's safe to say that most American immigrants did not come to this country primarily for religious purposes.

I don't say that in any way to minimize the influence of religion on immigration. I simply mean to point out the remarkably high level of religious commitment that exists in America today in light of the diverse backgrounds of our predecessors. The popularity of religion in America today is even more astounding considering the decline of religious belief in much of the rest of the world as intellectual secularism has grown to displace it. There is clearly a very vocal and influential secularist influence in the United States; but you can see by the Gallup poll that its influence seems way out of proportion with its true numerical strength. True secularists—those who don't believe in any form of religion—make up less than 10 percent of the total population of the country. But as the core group waging the battle against entanglement of church and state, they seem to carry far more weight than a 10 percent minority. Their ability to repeatedly challenge the government on this issue, keep it squarely in the public eye, and almost always win, would lead you to conclude they were in the majority.

For example, we just passed through the 2004 Christmas season in which there was a great uproar over the use of the word "Christmas" in public. Many Christmas programs and concerts scheduled to take place in public schools were cancelled or modified as school officials tried to mollify critics and walk the politically correct line. Even the National Christmas Tree that appears annually on the grounds of the United States Capitol was renamed the National Holiday Tree to avoid offending non-Christians. This name change surely seems overboard to me and many others. Will the next step in political correctness be renaming the weeping willow tree the emotionally sensitive tree so as not to offend the teary-eyed among us? Kidding aside, these episodes provide some insight into the strength and ability of the secular movement to impose its agenda on the rest of us. These episodes also make clear the over-eagerness of the Christian community to modify traditions in an effort to not offend non-Christian fellow citizens. Walking the line between standing up for your beliefs and respecting the beliefs of others has never been a more difficult walk than at the present time.

The poll also gives a good indication of why the issue of separation of church and state is so difficult to resolve. Two of the principles upon which our government is founded seem to be at odds with one another. On the one hand, our Constitution enforces separation of church and state, and on the other hand, government is staffed by elected representatives and career employees who are for the most part very religious. The total pool of government workers is large enough that we can assume it's statistically equivalent to the general population. According to the earlier referenced poll, that means that religion is either important or very important to 85 percent of government employees. Furthermore, fully 85 percent are Christian. You can begin to see why this is a never-ending struggle. Our founders created a system in which religion was to be entirely separate from government, but the government is staffed and operated for the most part by citizens with deep commitments to Christianity. Is it any surprise that it's difficult to keep the two separate? My objective over the course of the next few chapters is to provide some insight into why separation of church and state is so important and to express my opinion on when the line that should separate church and state has been crossed.

In God We Trust

A truly unbiased observer would find it difficult to conclude that our government really practices separation of church and state. Sure, the Constitution clearly indicates that the government is to function independent of any religion, but the current practice of this principle is quite far from the theory articulated by our Founding Fathers. Indications of the entanglement of religion and government are all around us. Probably the most pervasive example is the slogan found on our currency: "In God We Trust." It's inscribed on every coin and printed on every bill produced by the government of the United States. We handle currency every day without thinking of the religious sentiment conveyed with each monetary transaction. While currency might be the most pervasive example, there are many other examples of the intersection of religion and government. Everyday, in courthouses across the land, witnesses are sworn in prior to giving testimony. They pledge to tell the truth, the whole truth and nothing but the truth, while their left hand is placed on a Christian Bible. Every day in classrooms throughout the country, school children recite a Pledge of Allegiance to our flag, which refers to the United States as "one nation, under God." Every day that the United States Senate or House of Representatives is in session, the sessions begin with a prayer. Likewise, every Supreme Court session begins with prayer. When a president of the United States repeats the oath of office administered by the Chief Justice of the Supreme Court, he is required by law to conclude with the phrase "so help me God." And I think it's highly likely that every president of the United States has closed most public speeches with the phrase "may God bless America."

The list could go on and on, but the point is hopefully already made. How do we reconcile these seemingly religious government practices with the principle of separation of church and state? The simple answer is maybe we can't. Maybe we aren't practicing what the Founding Fathers preached. That would certainly be the conclusion of many blue voters. But most red voters, and a surprisingly large number of American historians, would argue that we are acting in perfect harmony with the principles established by the Founding Fathers. So, which side is right? There is no simple answer to that question. It's almost certain that a debate such as this one—a debate that has lasted for more than two centuries—persists because each side can make a good case for its position. If one side had a substantially better argument than the other, over such a long period of time, the better argument would clearly prevail. The problem is that both sides have relatively equal claim on the truth, and it has been that way from the beginning of this debate.

This case of governmental split personality was established when two very different documents were created by our Founding Fathers—the Declaration of Independence and the Constitution of the United States. The Declaration was written to formalize the fact that the Thirteen Colonies were separating from England. The principles affirmed in the Declaration are so revered, inspirational and quintessentially American that most of us are able to recite at least some of them from memory. I have cited the most familiar lines from the Declaration several times in the course of this document:

> "We hold these truths to be self-evident, that all men are created equal, that they are endowed by their Creator with certain unalienable rights, that among those are life, liberty and the pursuit of happiness. That to secure these rights, Governments are instituted among men...."

This sentence and a half—comprised of only 45 words—is likely the most often quoted passage by anyone seeking to express a concise articulation of American values. It doesn't really matter much that these 45 words represent only a very small portion of the complete Declaration of Independence. The remainder of the document continues at great length to enumerate the specific grievances the colonies had with England. These words have long been forgotten and rightly so. They were specific reasons for a war settled long ago and the circumstances are no longer applicable to us. But the opening statements are timeless. Today these sentiments ring as true and as inspirational as they did the day they were written. They are the philosophical underpinning of American culture. And in this profound statement of principles the Founding Fathers expressed their belief that the rights of life, liberty and happiness are given to us by our Creator. It's impossible to read this in any other way. The Declaration of Independence unequivocally states that God is the source and giver of these rights. Thus God was entangled in American politics right from the start.

Now move forward 11 years to the writing and ratification of the Constitution of the United States. The objective of the Constitution was very different from the objective of the Declaration of Independence. It was both a blueprint for how the new government would be organized and an establishment of principles upon which the organized government would function. As an example of the first objective, the Constitution established three branches of government—legislative, executive and judicial. As examples of the second objective, the Constitution established a balance of power between the branches of government, implemented a trial-by-jury judicial process, and guaranteed individual rights through a series of amendments called the Bill of Rights. In many ways the Constitution was the logical extension of the Declaration of Independence. It gave body to the bare skeleton of rights described in the opening sentences of the Declaration. But nowhere in the Constitution is there any acknowledgement of God as the author of these rights. In fact, there are no references to God anywhere in the document, and furthermore, the Constitution only addresses the subject of religion in two places. The first reference is in Article VI:

> The Senators and Representatives before mentioned, and the members of the several state legislatures, and all executive and judicial officers, both of the United States and of the several states, shall be bound by oath or affirmation, to support this Constitution; but no religious test shall ever be required as a qualification to any office or public trust under the United States.

And the second, more familiar statement, which is found in the Bill of Rights, establishes the principle of separation of church and state:

> Congress shall make no law respecting an establishment of religion, or prohibiting the free exercise thereof....

The intent of the Constitution to ensure separation of church and state is abundantly clear. The omission of God from the Constitution could not have been a mere oversight. It had to be the result of very specific intent and likely required diligent effort on the part of the Founding Fathers to avoid the more natural inclination of the time to make God a full partner in government. The founding documents of nearly all other governments of the western world at that time—including the state constitutions of the 13 states that would be ratifying the Constitution of the United States—almost always included a grandiose preamble that attributed the establishment and powers of the government to God. Most are written in a style similar to the opening paragraph of the Declaration of Independence. In fact, the authors of the Declaration were certainly influenced by their previous exposure to similar sentiments in their home state charters or constitutions. This practice was and is so pervasive that it continues to this very day. For example, the current constitutions of arguably the two most secular of all the states in the United States have the following preambles:

- We The People of the State of New York, grateful to Almighty God for our Freedom, in order to secure its blessings, do establish this Constitution.

- We, the People of the State of California, grateful to Almighty God for our freedom, in order to secure and perpetuate its blessings, do establish this Constitution.

New York's constitution existed at the birth of this country. California's was created many decades later, indicating how natural, habitual and ingrained the practice of including God in government charters has been even up to quite recent times. In fact, most of the original references to God in state constitutions remain to this very day. On top of that, most of the original state constitutions didn't limit themselves only to acknowledging God as the source and giver of individual rights. Many required state officeholders to pledge allegiance to some sort of religious faith. Ironically, the state of Massachusetts for many years had such a requirement in its constitution. It's hard to believe that the home state of the most well known benefactors of American religious freedom—the Pilgrims and Puritans—was itself intolerant of religious diversity. But this wasn't a rarity; it was the norm. Fortunately, all requirements for a profession of religious faith by officeholders were dropped over the course of the 19th century, bringing state constitutions into compliance with the national constitution.

If such thinking was standard practice at the time, how did God get left out of the Constitution of the United States? The total absence of any reference to God, and the clear separation of church and state, had to be a willful and striking declaration of principle. I don't believe it could have been an accident. The fundamental reason for this departure from tradition is obvious. After all, this country was initially founded in part as a haven for religious freedom and toleration. It was settled and organized by people who were seeking a different way and one of the primary differences they sought was the right to freely practice a religion of their choice, not to be forced to observe a designated state religion. The authors of the Constitution were therefore obligated to turn away from the tradition of invoking God as a founding partner of government and to take the additional steps necessary to ensure that the United States would never establish a state religion. These were essential founding principles and it seems to me that they were implemented with great discipline in spite of the natural inclination at the time to do otherwise.

I think it was an admirable triumph of common sense government over personal inclination and faith. There has been much debate over the years concerning the true depth of religious conviction held by our Founding Fathers. If their writing reflects true feelings concerning faith in God, then surely many, if not most, were deeply religious. On the other hand, references to God in writing or speech in those days was an expected rhetorical enhancement and not necessarily reflective of a true commitment. Books have been written and careers spent attempting to determine the truth in this regard. It's an interesting pursuit for a variety of reasons. If the Founding Fathers were deeply religious, it is interesting to consider the remarkable restraint and foresight they exhibited in drafting a Constitution that ensured freedom of worship for all. If they weren't deeply religious, it's interesting to consider how so many have been fooled into thinking they were. Fortunately, for the purpose of this discussion, the answers to these interesting questions are really not relevant. Regardless of their own personal feelings concerning religion, they created a Constitution that forbids the state from imposing any religion on its citizens and grants each citizen the freedom to worship as he or she chooses. This is the law as contained in the Constitution of the United States and the intent is clear to anyone who reads the document.

As Americans, we should respect both the Declaration of Independence and the Constitution. But they were written for very different purposes. The Declaration is in essence a spiritual document and the Constitution is a legal document. This bi-polar nature of our founding documents is the reason this great debate concerning separation of church and state persists. Each side is supported by one of the documents. Those who believe that the hand of God needs to be recognized in government cite the spirituality found in the Declaration of Independence and by other private and public documents of our Founding Fathers. Those who favor strict separation of religion and state are legally correct because the Constitution of the United States, the law of the land, is on their side. It's actually quite surprising that the battle has lasted this long. The law is clearly on the side of absolute separation of church and state, and the law will ultimately prevail. Of this there is no doubt. The Supreme Court issues decisions based on compliance with the Constitution, not on compliance with the Declaration of Independence. It would take a Constitutional amendment to change this course, and we all know that will not happen on this issue. Any activity of government that can be judged by a reasonable person as establishment of religion—or even the promotion of religion—will ultimately be judged unconstitutional by the Supreme Court. The court has no other choice with the existing Constitution. And as this relentless march to total separation progresses, it will continue to frustrate those who want more of God in government.

There are two reasons that explain why God has not already been entirely eradicated from the government of the United States. First, as I have already pointed out, statements of a religious nature in the Declaration of Independence confound the issue. And second, the American people are intensely religious. On the first point, even the Founding Fathers found that it's not always easy to practice what you preach. Though they intellectually understood the need for separation, they and their fellow citizens were not vigilant in enforcing separation. Old habits were very difficult to break. The country was overwhelmingly religious and overwhelmingly Christian. So it didn't really upset the vast majority of Americans when the God of Christianity got considerably entangled with government. Unfortunately, this perpetuated the problem and allowed its roots to grow very deep. By the time the first major court challenges concerning separation of church and state were settled in this past century, the practice was so entrenched that court decisions in favor of separation were shocking to the general public. God and state had been bound together for so long that everyone assumed the entanglement would be legally justified. A good portion of the public continues to be concerned as court decision after court decision is settled in favor of separation. This concern is not surprising in a population in which 85 percent of us think religion is very important. It's not easy to standby and witness God being pushed out of government when the push is administered by such a small minority of the total population.

I number myself among the majority of Americans who believe religion is a very important part of our lives. But in my opinion, we are very fortunate to have a legal foundation that ensures government cannot dictate or require specific religious faith and cannot interfere with the religious faith of any citizen. The Founding Fathers weren't only politically correct for incorporating these principles into the Constitution; they were also incredibly wise to do so. Separation of church and state is essential. If you have any doubts about that, consider the alternatives. What if we had a state religion that was imposed on every citizen? It is of course unimaginable—even un-American—to consider it. But short of that, what if the state favored one religion above all others? How would you feel if a religious organization other than your own was given "Most Favored Status?" If you are not a member of the Christian faith, you might believe that is exactly what has happened in spite of the protections in the Constitution that were supposed to prevent it. Personally, I don't think the entanglement of Christianity and the United States government has done any real harm to any other religious organization. In fact, overall, the moral influence has undoubtedly been a good thing. That's probably the primary reason that the entanglement has lasted so long. It was doing much more good than harm. Nevertheless, if we are serious about practicing what we preach, our government should be supportive of all legitimate religious practice and not favor any particular faith. Thank goodness—or if you are so inclined, thank God—that such protection exists. At times, the nit-picking of those who insist on total separation of not just church and state but of religion and state can seem awfully silly. But the protection the Constitution affords all of us to worship as we please is well worth enduring a little bit of nit-picking.

Don't get me wrong. I'm not trying to encourage additional legal efforts to rid our government of any and all religious connections. Many, if not most, of the secularly driven initiatives that seek to totally remove God from government are excessive and over the top. Consider the examples I cited at the beginning of this chapter. They are just a few of the many signs of the entanglement of religion and government that are around us on a daily basis. All have been, and will continue to be, challenged by secular forces who wish to see them completely removed from government. Most of us throw our hands up in disbelief that anyone would even challenge such minor and inconsequential incursions of religion in government. After all, how can having the inscription "In God We Trust" on our currency possibly be considered the imposition of state religion, or as an expression of intolerance toward any religion? It's a reference to a generic God, not necessarily the God of Christianity or any other specific religion. I seriously doubt that anyone has been converted to religion by an ambiguous slogan on a coin. I personally find the slogan a source of humor not religion. On the rare occasions when I have actually read the slogan it reminds me of a commentary that I heard at some point in my life, "Americans might trust God—but they worship money." I must have heard it from a Frenchman. No matter the source, it's a nice way to put in perspective the innocuous nature of any religious commentary on coins. And how about the other examples cited at the beginning of this chapter? Does the practice of swearing in a court witness by having them place their hand on a Bible really have any religious significance at all? It's nothing more than a process that serves to emphasize the significance of the testimony. It's not a form of preaching, proselytizing, or the imposition of Christianity on the witness or anyone else. The same is true with oaths of office of all types, prayers in Congress and prayers in the Supreme Court. None of these activities are really at odds with the intent of the Constitution. But if the courts continue to find that some or all of them are, we ought to happily go along with their conclusions. It's a small price to pay for the religious freedom and tolerance we are so fortunate to have.

School Prayer

School prayer is the primary combat zone in the battle over separation of church and state. It makes perfect sense that it is. The public school system is the most pervasive instrument of government by any form of measurement. It reaches into every community and touches nearly all of us at one time or another, first as students and perhaps later as parents of students. A typical child spends six or more hours a day at school for nine months each year over the course of 13 years. And these many hours are not inconsequential. Theoretically, the time is spent developing academic and life skills, which will have a tremendous influence and impact on the child's quality of life. And nothing is of more concern to parents than the development and success of their children. Government touches our lives in many ways, but no other government function can match the influence of the public school system. It's only natural that the battle over separation of church and state rages most strongly there.

The debate over whether or not prayer ought to be allowed in public schools is not new. It has been underway since the advent of the public school system. Initially, public school administrators were not shy about including religious content in the curriculum. In most early schools, reading from the Protestant Bible and reciting the Protestant version of The Lord's Prayer was common practice. The Protestant branches of the Christian church were so predominant in the early years of American history that such practices didn't even raise any eyebrows. Decades later, as Catholic immigrants poured into the country, a growing Catholic student population was responsible for the first challenge to school-led Bible study and prayer. Catholics objected to the use of the Protestant Bible and the Protestant version of The Lord's Prayer. Catholic students and parents were not against Bibles and prayers in school. In fact, the dispute initially was over which Bible and prayer to use—Protestant or Catholic. There were many intense protests at the time, including riots in Philadelphia in 1844, resulting in serious injury and even death to some of the participants

Today, thankfully, the lives of students and parents are not in peril over this debate, but emotions on both sides still run high. These emotions are further inflamed by the widespread belief that the quality of public education in general is declining to perilously low levels. In some communities the decline has reached crisis proportions. And the decline is not only academic. Discipline and morality have also suffered precipitous declines. For those who support the practice of prayer in school, the start of this steady decline in the quality of public education can be traced back to the early 1960s. In their minds, it's not just a coincidence that the start of this decline can be linked to a seminal Supreme Court decision concerning prayer in public schools. In 1962, in Engel v. Vitale, the Court ruled that a prayer written by a New York state board of education, which was required recitation in school classrooms throughout the district, was essentially government promotion of religion and violated the establishment of religion clause of the First Amendment. Therefore, the Court ruled that the practice must end. If prayers written by the school board were illegal, it was only a matter of time until the Bible and The Lord's Prayer would suffer a similar fate. The Court accomplished this rejection within the same year with a decision in Albington Township Pennsylvania School District v. Schempp. And it didn't end with these two decisions. The Court has taken on this issue in a variety of forms over the past 40 years, and the decisions have all been consistent—no school-sponsored prayer or scripture in public schools. One of the more recent cases, decided in 2000, dealt with the issue of prayer at school athletic events. In Santa Fe Independent School District v.

Doe, the Supreme Court ruled that public school athletic events are school sponsored activities and must adhere to the same restriction—no prayers. Similarly, another recent case ended the practice of prayer at graduation ceremonies. In essence, over the course of the past 40 years, school-sponsored prayer has effectively been banished from the public schools.

Many parents are obviously distressed by the Court's decisions, but quite frankly, the Court is not to blame. Any rational reading of the Constitution would lead to the same conclusion. You don't have to pass a bar exam to understand that. It is in fact surprising that public schools were able to continue these practices for such a long period of time. Unfortunately, that long period of habitual—but illegal—practice left the impression that a right of school-sponsored prayer has been taken away when in fact the right never existed in the first place. More importantly, not one citizen's individual rights have been changed one iota by these rulings. The Court did not eliminate prayer and scripture reading from anyone's life. It eliminated school-sponsored prayer and school-sponsored reading of scripture. "School sponsored" is the operative qualifier. The ban isn't on the practice of religion, it is on school sponsorship of religion. A school cannot be seen as an advocate of any religious denomination. Though a school as an institution is under this restriction, every student in that school continues to have the right to voluntarily pray or read the Bible on school property during free time. Prayer and scripture study can even be allowed in groups or clubs that meet during non-class times, as long as any student groups formed for other purposes are granted the same access and support. The Court has ruled that schools can even teach from and about the Bible as long as it is part of an objective study of religion, has a legitimate educational purpose and the instructor presents the material in an unbiased fashion. Given the difficulty of ensuring that an instructor can make an unbiased presentation of religious material, school boards and administrators have wisely shied away from offering classes of a religious nature in public schools. Though this approach is prudent and necessary, it has deepened the problem by perpetuating a myth that none of these things are allowed in school.

To me, banning school-sponsored prayer is both good law and common sense. I remember my own experience as a public school student in the 1960s when school-sponsored prayer at athletic events and other non-classroom activities was still regularly practiced. Coaches and administrators made an honest effort to involve as many local ministers in the practice as possible. But non-Christian prayers were never offered and I don't recall any Catholic priest every participating even though we had many Catholic children in the community. And though it was never expressed, I would imagine that the non-Christian and Catholic students were both discouraged by the slight and perhaps even offended by any doctrinal expressions in the prayers that were inconsistent with their own faith. Though I am of Christian faith, my own reaction to the prayers could best be classified as ambivalent. They were never offered by an official from my particular denomination, and contrary to the uniform picture of Christianity that many Christians would like to paint, there are significant doctrinal differences between the various denominations of Christianity. The Christian majority is anything but a monolith. On the surface Christianity has the illusion of unity, but beneath the surface, the various denominations exist precisely because they worship Jesus Christ differently. If there weren't significant differences between the various Christian denominations they would have no reason to exist independently. It's true that all of the Christian denominations are descendants of the same parent religion, but 2,000 years of differing experiences has created a very diverse Christian family. There are differences in how prayer is offered, where and when prayer is appropriate and what doctrine is expressed in prayer. It might seem like nitpicking, but doctrinal references in prayer can contribute to a child's understanding of the nature of God and what He expects of us. A Christian prayer that expresses doctrine different from the doctrine taught to the child at home or in his or her church can be confusing to someone still in the developmental stages of acquiring faith. I seriously doubt that school-sponsored prayers made any real difference in the religious choices of students who participated in them, but for the sake of ensuring that school-sponsored prayer did not transform itself subtly into school-sponsored religion, I am in full support of the ban imposed by the Court. The best way to preserve the depth and diversity of religion that exists in our country today is to ensure that we promote our faith of choice at home and insist that our public schools provide an environment that respects all faiths and denigrates none.

The American public reacted so negatively to the Supreme Court ruling on school-sponsored prayer in 1963 that President John Kennedy felt compelled to issue the following public statement concerning the decision:

> "We have in this case a very easy remedy, and that is to pray ourselves. And I would think it would be a welcome reminder to every American family that we can pray a good deal more at home, we can attend our churches with a good deal more fidelity, and we can make the true meaning of prayer much more important in the lives of our children."

Kennedy's words are right on the mark. Faith is a right and a responsibility that should be nurtured at home and not tampered with in the public schools. I find it a considerable irony that those clamoring the loudest to re-establish prayer in school are the very same people who most likely are also clamoring to get government in general out of their lives. On the one hand, they are asking the government, through the public school system, to intrude in the most personal and fundamental of matters, faith. And on the other hand, they want government to stay out of their lives on issues of far less importance. This is most inconsistent, but quite understandable. All parents recognize that decisions regarding faith are among the most important decisions an individual can make. Parents desire only the best for their children. They hope that prayer in school will be that little edge that keeps the flame of faith burning in their children. Those who advocate school-sponsored prayer might be well intended, but for all of the reasons I've already articulated, school-sponsored prayer has more potential for harm than good.

President Bush introduced the concept of an "ownership society" in the recently concluded presidential election campaign. The principle behind the concept is that citizens who own something will manage it more effectively than government can and that personal ownership will breathe new life into the declining American spirit of self-reliance and forward progress. I support the idea 100 percent. The concept has great merit and is philosophically sound. Re-establishing the preeminence of the principle of self-reliance is essential to maintaining the American way of life. But I haven't heard President Bush or anyone else use this terminology in reference to personal faith. Of all the potential assets we might own, none have any greater importance than the asset of personal faith. Faith should be at the top of any list of assets that are to be owned by citizens of an "ownership society." It's time for those who promote religious practice in schools to redirect the energy and effort they are spending on that battle into the development of personal and family faith instead. To put it bluntly, they need to step up to the plate themselves instead of expecting public schools to do it for them.

In or Of the Public Square

Americans hold many different opinions about when, where and how religion should be acknowledged in public, and those differences of opinion always seem to be more pronounced during the months of November and December in the days leading up to the Christmas holiday. It shouldn't be surprising that a major Christian holiday would be widely recognized and celebrated in a nation that is 85% Christian. Even many non-Christians recognize and celebrate Christmas as a secular holiday, focusing on Santa Claus, Christmas trees and gift giving instead of celebrating the birth of Jesus Christ. Still, whenever December rolls around, you can always count on hearing several stories of individuals or groups taking legal action to stop the public display of a Christian nativity scene or other religious symbol of the Christmas holiday. But there seemed to be more of this kind of protest than usual in December 2004. Some would likely attribute it to disgruntled secularists expressing frustration that was aggravated by the re-election of President Bush. But I don't think these protests were a one-off experience. I believe that what happened last December is part of an intensifying trend that will continue to grow over the next several years. In fact, as we enter the 2005 Christmas season it appears that we are in for quite a battle. Well in advance of the Christmas holiday, John Gibson, popular host of "The Big Story" on the Fox News Channel, published his latest book, "The War on Christmas: How the Liberal Plot to Ban the Sacred Christian Holiday is Worse Than You Thought." It rapidly moved into the upper reaches of the Amazon best seller list as frustrated Christians embraced the theme and prepared themselves for another contentious Christmas season. And brisk sales of Gibson's book are not the only indication that many Christians are seething over the secular attacks on Christmas, as evidenced by this recent news story:

> It's weeks before Thanksgiving but already interest groups are preparing for an intense year of conflict over Christmas observances by cities and public schools, with one conservative group lining up hundreds of attorneys to work on the issue.
>
> This week, the Alliance Defense Fund, a Christian legal group based in Scottsdale, Arizona, announced that its 800 cooperating attorneys have volunteered to handle without fee complaints about "improper attempts to censor the celebration of Christmas in schools and on public property."
>
> The topic is also the subject of a polemic by the Fox News Channel's John Gibson that is selling briskly: "The War on Christmas: How the Liberal Plot to Ban the Sacred Christian Holiday Is Worse Than You Thought." Gibson, who calls himself a "nonpracticing Christian," notes that his Jewish son researched the book. He says agitation against Christmas observance comes primarily from "secularists, so-called humanists, trial lawyers, cultural relativists and liberal, guilt-wracked Christians."
>
> —Richard N. Ostling, Associated Press, Friday, November 4, 2005

It might appear that the Christian army will easily win this battle. After all, Christianity is the religion of choice for 85 percent of the country, and with thousands of lawyers prepared to man the trenches, how can the small opposing forces made up of non-Christians and secularists possibly prevail? Ordinarily an 85 to 15 margin would signify certain victory. But in this case, if I were a betting man, I would bet that the secular lions once again defeat the Christians in the lion's den. How? We must first recognize that even though Christians are fed-up with the status quo, secularists are even more passionate and determined in their cause. The non-Christians involved in these actions are responding to what they believe is an ever-increasing melding of Christian doctrine with government practice. To them, President Bush's unapologetic, public expression of his personal faith is evidence of this melding process, and in the court of public opinion, the non-Christians submit Bush's outspoken faith as people's exhibit number one.

But secularist passion alone does not fully explain how the massive Christian majority goes down in flames every year on this issue. Gibson hit the nail on the head when he enumerated the forces arrayed against Christmas. The last group he enumerated, "liberal, guilt-wracked Christians," is really the key to understanding the strength of the anti-Christmas forces. Christians have no one to blame but themselves for this relentless march against Christmas. An old and familiar line perfectly describes the situation Christians are in: "We have met the enemy, and the enemy is us."

Why are many Christians so "guilt-wracked" that they are rendered ineffective in defending Christmas? The source of the guilt is primarily a concern that anything a member of the Christian majority might say or do could offend any of a number of non-Christian minorities. If you have been employed by any major corporation over the past 20 years or so, you will understand one of the significant cultural forces that have heightened this sensitivity to non-Christian minorities. Today, most large corporations have officers and staffs dedicated to ensuring respect for diversity in the work force. I'm not complaining. For far too long there was little or no respect for diversity in American business. Conformity, not diversity, was expected and rewarded. I think this recent emphasis on diversity is not only good business, but good, period. However, one of the side effects created by this effort to ensure equality is an almost over-sensitivity to diversity. At times I even get the impression that it is more than over-sensitivity. It's more like fear—fear that anything we say or do is likely to offend someone. Conversely, while the majority of the country is retreating out of sensitivity or fear, minorities have been further emboldened to assert their minority causes. The collision of emboldened minorities with an extremely sympathetic and apologetic majority has resulted in strained relations and some unnecessary retreats from common sense. The story I related in an earlier chapter of the National Christmas Tree transformed into the National Holiday Tree, is a good example of the majority trying to preemptively avoid a potential conflict through politically correct behavior. No legal action was taken to have the name changed. So far as we know, congressional leadership made the decision without pressure from non-Christian organizations. Avoiding the possibility of offending others is certainly a nice sentiment, but most of us think this was an example of being overly concerned. In a similar vein, perhaps you heard the stories of public school authorities preemptively changing the name of the perennial school Christmas program to avoid offending non-Christian students and families. Your local school's annual Christmas program has likely been replaced by the more politically correct annual Holiday program. And we have all likely experienced the agonizing process of selecting an inoffensive holiday card to send to non-Christian friends at Christmas time.

As Americans we have always been known for our ability to get things done without long debate and procrastination. We are the envy of the world in terms of productivity mainly because we don't mess around over-thinking everything, and we don't get overly discouraged by long odds against potential success. Practicality and optimism are wonderful traits to have, but they also cause us to go overboard from time to time. I suspect that's what has happened to some extent with our current fixation on political correctness. We are so busy being politically correct that we haven't thought enough about whether or not it even makes sense. That has certainly happened in the case of public religious expression. The pendulum has swung too far to the side of removing religion from public life. It needs to start swinging back to the middle.

Both law and common sense can provide us with the guidance necessary for the pendulum to end up in the right place. The applicable law is all contained within the First Amendment to the Constitution:

> Congress shall make no law respecting an establishment of religion, or prohibiting the free exercise thereof; or abridging the freedom of speech, or of the press; or the right of the people peaceably to assemble, and to petition the government for a redress of grievances.

The Supreme Court has determined that religious displays are expressions of speech. Therefore, anything anyone wants to say or display relative to a legitimate religion is always acceptable and protected by law when on private, not government property. When on government property, the Court has determined that religious displays or religious speech are not allowed if they are instigated by agents or employees of the government. Such activity by government employees would violate the "establishment of religion" clause of the First Amendment. However, religious displays and speech on public property are allowed when instigated by private citizens who are not employees of the government. There are a couple of tests a religious display must pass to be acceptable in the public square:

- The public area (park, town square, plaza, government building, street corner, school building, sidewalk, etc.) must have been opened up for public expression to other civic and religious groups. In other words it can't be withheld for one specific group over another. All must be equally welcome.

- Government cannot endorse the religious display or speech.

A simple way to describe what is allowed and what is not allowed is contained in the following statement: It is OK for religious displays to be "in" the public square, but it is not OK for those displays to be "of" the public square. The source and endorsement of the display must be private and cannot give the appearance of endorsement from the government.

It seems to me that the Supreme Court's decision is very consistent with a common sense interpretation of the First Amendment. Why then do we have such difficulty any time a significant religious holiday is recognized in a public setting? I've already alluded to two of the primary reasons. First, the majority is bending over backwards to avoid either offending minorities or violating the law as they understand it. Second, minorities have been emboldened both by success in the workplace and by the willingness of the majority to give-in without a fight. The current practice of almost always giving-in to a non-Christian minority is often wrong. We can't promote diversity as long as it comes from the minority on the one hand and then with the other hand suppress the diversity represented by the majority. American principles and law are designed to protect minority rights, but not at the expense of the rights of the majority. The situation is unfortunate because we would all benefit greatly from a more aggressive use of the public square for open and honest expression, not only of faith, but of other fundamental beliefs as well. Encouraging free speech is in fact the best way to preserve diversity. The current solution—suppressing the voice of the majority—has exactly the opposite effect. It creates a false sense that diversity is being celebrated, while beneath the surface the majority viewpoint is resentfully suppressed. If we really believe that strength comes from diversity, we shouldn't discourage any part of the population from freely expressing their beliefs, including those in the majority. Only through open dialogue can we ensure that others are not ignorant of what we stand for. Ignorance is the primary cause of intolerance; and stifling religious speech in public will only serve to increase intolerance between religious organizations.

Restoring the appropriate balance in the use of the public square for religious purposes will require that we are more diligent in ensuring that what we do is "in" the public square and not "of" the public square. Violations of that principle are the cause of our current situation. Whenever we find government endorsing religion in the public square, we should insist that government get out of the business of religion. We should also insist that government open up the public square to all religious organizations, not favoring one over another. If these conditions are met, the public square provides a great opportunity for education, which will ultimately increase respect and tolerance. Let's have more religion "in" the public square, and less of the intolerance that attempts to suppress it.

Church and Citizen

In 1960, John Kennedy was elected as the first non-Protestant president of the United States. He ended a streak of 33 straight Protestant presidents dating back to the beginning of U. S. history. Any other winning streak—including the New York Yankee dynasties—pales in comparison. The fact that it took 172 years to elect a non-Protestant president says a lot about America. It's indicative not only of the dominance of the Protestant form of Christianity but also of the pervasive nature of Protestant thought and values in our country. Those values were and still are the foundation of American culture. At the time of his election, Kennedy's Roman Catholic faith was a big deal. It was never discussed openly by his opponent Richard Nixon, but it was certainly used against Kennedy by Nixon's supporters. We've come so far as a nation in terms of respect for religious diversity over the last 40 years that it's difficult in this day and age to comprehend the outright fear and hostility that existed in 1960 between Catholic and Protestant Christians.

I can recall my own experience with this conflict while attending a rural public school in a predominantly Protestant community. The most visible and frequent reminder of the rift occurred every Friday at lunch time. Friday was the one day of the week that the school lunch menu showed any sign of variety. Protestant students were offered the usual mashed potatoes and beef gravy while Catholic students received a special meal featuring fish sticks so they could observe the Catholic practice of abstaining from meat on Fridays. Nearly every Friday, there was sure to be a verbal exchange between the Protestant and Catholic students in the lunch line. The Catholics were always the target of the abuse but were not bashful in offering the same in return. As such youthful exchanges go, it was mostly in good fun. But there was more than a grain of truth underlying the exchanges. I can even remember a handful of times when tempers flared and fist fights followed. Given the strength of the animosity expressed by so many of the children, you can well imagine what parents were saying at home. Intolerance and disrespect had to be quite strong at home to have filtered into the psyches of school children otherwise notorious for ignoring parental conversation.

My own recollections date from the mid- to late 1960s, so you can well imagine what it was like nearly a decade earlier at the time Kennedy was running for president. Protestant organizations and prominent Protestant clerics issued public statements against Kennedy, insisting that as a Catholic he would be obligated to blindly follow direction from the Pope. They tried to make it sound as if electing Kennedy was akin to electing the Pope himself. Derogatory anti-Catholic literature was produced and widely distributed throughout the country. Kennedy was graceful, artful and disarming in how he dealt with the issue, as he always was when he found himself in a tight spot. As an example, consider this statement made during the campaign:

> "I am not the Catholic candidate for president. I am the Democratic Party's candidate for president, who happens also to be Catholic. I do not speak for my church on public matters—and the church does not speak for me."

Kennedy won, but it was one of the closest winning margins in history. Undoubtedly, his Catholic faith played a significant role in keeping the election close. He likely would have won by a landslide if he had been Protestant and not Catholic. His victory not only opened the door for other non-Protestant presidential candidates, but I believe it also started the long overdue process of building respect between the various religious organizations in this country. We certainly have come a long way on that road in the past 40 years and ought to be proud of the progress we've made.

Conversely, the lack of respect between religious and secular, or in other words non-religious, groups is another story. It seems to me that the relationship between secularists and religionists has deteriorated significantly during this same period of time. Consider the following opinion that appeared in The Baltimore Sun on March 16, 2003. It's only one example of the many that could be given, but it is representative of the general animosity and fear that secularists have of President Bush's reliance on faith. Though written by one Gordon Livingston, under the title "True Believer's Moral Certainty Leads Us Astray," it's certainly a sentiment shared by many secularists:

> As the United States prepares to launch a pre-emptive war, it is worth looking at what is driving President Bush to ignore the reservations of most of our allies and at least half of the American people in pursuit of his obsession with Iraq.
>
> The answer clearly lies in the combination of the myth of the Old West and Southern religion that informs his every action. The former evokes images of the lonely gunfighter as a force for good; the latter provides a moral justification for the constructive use of violence.
>
> Deeply religious people are, by definition, certain that they are right about life's large questions. It is in the nature of religious belief to have complete confidence about the (un-provable) existence of a particular deity and assurance in a specific interpretation of some set of religious writings that purport to reveal God's will.

This is not an isolated example. I think any objective observer would agree that President Bush has been ceaselessly criticized for invoking faith and prayer in his decision-making process. And unlike the "whispering campaign" concerning Kennedy's faith, concerns about President Bush's faith are expressed openly by Democratic leadership and the mainstream media. Every major news organization has covered the topic several times. For example, the two primary weekly news magazines—Time and Newsweek—have had cover articles on this topic during the course of Bush's first term. The Newsweek cover article from March 10, 2003, was entitled "Bush and God." The subtitle read:

> A higher calling: It is his defining journey—from reveler to revelation. A biography of his faith, and how he wields it as he leads a nation on the brink of war.

To be fair, this is a brief excerpt from an article that covers a lot of ground. The full article describes the evolution of President Bush's faith and its effect on his political life. The article does have a certain level of balance about it. But expressions of the secular concerns of being led by someone with deep religious faith are found throughout, including this example:

> Still, faith helps Bush pick a course and not look back. He talks regularly to pastors, and loves to hear that people are praying for him. As he describes it, his faith is not complex. In recent weeks he has added a new note to his theme of the personal uses of faith, drawn from CBS. Now there is a sense of destiny that approaches the Calvinistic. "There is a fatalistic element," said David Frum, the author and former Bush speechwriter. "You do your best and accept that everything is in God's hands." The result is unflappability. "If you are confident that there is a God that rules the world," said Frum, "you do your best, and things will work out." But what some see as solidity, others view as a flammable mix of stubbornness and arrogance. "No one's allowed to second-guess, even when you should," said another former staffer.

If you strip away the subtlety of language, secularists fear that a religious president—like President Bush—might actually pursue an agenda consistent with his faith. And perhaps even more concerning to secularists, the president might even pray to God for guidance and believe to have received it. The thought of direction coming from a God, who secularists do not believe exists, is worrisome to them on two fronts. First, secularists believe it's irrational, or at best shallow, to believe in God. Second, secularists fear that a leader who thinks he receives direction from God may stop listening to counsel from his appointed advisors and others. Why listen to mere mortals when God is available for conversation? The second fear is clearly expressed in the two articles I have already cited. The first fear, in which secularists view President Bush as either delusional or intellectually challenged, is an even more commonly expressed opinion. To cite the most ironic of these expressions, his opponent John Kerry was quoted by Newsweek to have remarked after a Bush news conference, "I can't believe I am losing to this idiot." Of course the "idiot" won the election and got the last laugh. A less gracious man then President Bush might be well justified in asking Senator Kerry, "If I am an idiot and won the election, what does that say about your intellectual capability?" Much of the criticism of President Bush's intellect is the result of his occasional mangling of the English language, but don't be fooled that it is the only concern. We all know that the secularist view, which is magnified by a sympathetically secularist press, is that faith in God is a sign of a simple and a shallow mind. How could it be otherwise for a secularist? By its very definition, secularism rejects the existence of God because logic and intellect lead to the inevitable conclusion that God does not exist. Thus, anyone who believes in God must think illogically and fall short of the intellectual capability of any secularist.

President Bush should not feel singled out in this regard. Ironically, secularist fears started in earnest with the election of a very devout Democratic president, Jimmy Carter. Their fears intensified with the ascendancy of Ronald Reagan and were in hiatus during the relatively non-religious presidencies of George Bush the elder and Bill Clinton. Thus ironically, though John Kennedy's election accelerated the acceptance of non-Protestant candidates for elected office, secularist intolerance of office holders who are religious is on the upswing.

Secularists not only prefer that elected officials check their religion at the office door, but they also actually expect it to happen. It seems to me to be a very strange expectation and if it does occur, a very detrimental one as well. Every elected official comes to office equipped with a variety of skills, experiences and beliefs. Wouldn't it be silly to suggest that a newly elected official should abandon his or her academic training while in office? Or likewise, ignore life experiences that when considered might positively influence his or her decisions? It's more than silly. It's strange to suggest that our government leaders leave all or part of what makes them who they are at the door once elected to office. Indeed, they have theoretically been elected to office because of the very skills, experiences and values that comprise their personality and character.

It's even stranger still to expect that someone would leave true religious conviction at the door and govern as if religion had never existed in their life. For those who have deep religious faith, its principles are likely to be the most fundamental building blocks of that person's character. If someone truly believes in something, putting it aside to obtain a public office is not an option. If a person truly believes that praying to God is important, they should not stop praying to God, no matter what role they have in life. To do so would be a denial of the very faith they profess. In fact, we should be very concerned when the opposite occurs, when someone is actually willing to check their faith and values at the door. What kind of a person is it who says, "I am a member of a particular faith, and I attend church regularly. But don't worry because I will not let my faith influence my conduct in government service." Such insincerity ought to be troubling to all of us. A candidate who is willing to give a false impression of commitment to a religious faith is a candidate who is willing to do anything to get elected. You couldn't find a more clear-cut case of pandering to an electorate.

Fortunately, the vast majority of Americans have no problem seeing through such pandering. Though they might not agree with a particular candidate's religious faith, they do appreciate someone who is not afraid to stand up for what they believe in. I believe that kind of thinking played a very significant role in this past presidential election. There are many who disagree with President Bush on a variety of issues, especially the war in Iraq. But in the end, they voted for him in spite of the differences, primarily because he was willing to stand up for what he believes in. On the other hand, John Kerry undoubtedly lost many votes because of his flip-flopping—more formally described as pandering—on a variety of issues. "Flip-flopper" was a Republican charge that managed to stick because it was at least in part true. Kerry was quite willing to modify his stand on many issues if he felt it might attract additional voters. There are many Kerry-isms that could be cited, but probably one of the more blatant attempts at pandering was on the issue of abortion. First consider Kerry's comments at a pro-abortion rally in Washington, D.C. on April 23, 2004:

"If you need any motivation [to vote for me] let me give you three little words—the Supreme Court. More than 30 years after Roe v. Wade became the law of the land, it has never been more at risk than it is today. We are going to have a change in leadership in this country to protect the right of choice."

The remarks were expected. Senator Kerry's voting record is 100 percent pro-abortion. But contrast his remarks at the pro-abortion rally with his statement of personal belief about abortion that was given in the second presidential debate of 2004:

"First of all, I cannot tell you how deeply I respect the belief about life and when it begins. I'm a Catholic, raised a Catholic. I was an altar boy. Religion has been a huge part of my life. It helped lead me through a war, leads me today.

But I can't take what is an article of faith for me and legislate it for someone who doesn't share that article of faith, whether they be agnostic, atheist, Jew, Protestant, whatever. I can't do that.

But I can counsel people. I can talk reasonably about life and about responsibility. I can talk to people, as my wife Teresa does, about making other choices, and about abstinence, and about all these other things that we ought to do as a responsible society.

But as a president, I have to represent all the people in the nation. And I have to make that judgment.

Now, I believe that you can take that position and not be pro-abortion..."

The reference Kerry makes to an article of faith is a reference to the unconditional anti-abortion stand of his faith—the Roman Catholic Church. The inconsistency between these two statements is striking, and they are not isolated statements nor taken out of context. He has repeated them many times, and I am sure he would repeat them both again today if asked. In simple English, which is apparently somewhat beyond Kerry's capability to produce, he says that as a Catholic he supports his church in its belief that abortion is wrong. And though he would never attempt to impose his personal belief on others, he is obligated by his faith to "counsel" anyone who seeks an abortion not to do it. This is of course an appealing position to anyone who opposes abortion. But at the pro-abortion rally, clearly to attract pro-abortion voters, he promises to appoint only pro-abortion judges to the Supreme Court, an act that will ensure abortion remains legal. If he truly believed that abortion was wrong, wouldn't he appoint open-minded judges who might find legal grounds for overturning Roe v. Wade? Or perhaps he could really be true to his professed faith and sponsor an amendment to the Constitution that would take abortion entirely out of the hands of the Court.

I'm picking on Kerry only because he is the most recent example of a prominent elected official attempting to leave a professed religion at the door when entering elected office. Such behavior is in essence "not practicing what you preach." None of us are perfect enough to always practice what we preach, but there is a big difference between falling short of ideals and willfully ignoring expressed ideals for personal gain. To put it more bluntly, we tend to respect people who are trying to live up to standards, and we don't trust people who say they believe something yet make little or no effort to prove it.

When a religious citizen is elected to office, we should expect, even demand, that their religion does not get checked at the door. When an officer of government practices a particular faith it is not a separation of church and state issue. The Second Amendment is only violated if the government is used as a tool to promote the religion of the elected official. Sufficient checks and balances exist in our form of government that it is very unlikely that an official could successfully use government as a tool of religion. If it were to occur, a quick remedy would be found. Our system is incapable of tolerating it and is well equipped with the tools necessary to eradicate it. We should encourage every elected official to bring every personal tool they have acquired to office with them, whether it's academic training, personal experience or religious faith. Secular voters who fear faith in office have an alternative—the ballot box. They are free to vote for secular or moderately religious candidates. In the end, the will of the majority will determine whether the person elected is a person of faith or not. The current elitist mentality against faith that pervades both the political and media worlds is actually preventing voters from getting a more complete view of candidates. In this politically correct climate, candidates are forced to skirt around the issue of personal faith and avoid the negative media reaction it will undoubtedly unleash. Common sense would lead us to believe that just the opposite is necessary. We should know in great specificity the depth of a candidate's faith and the principles of that faith. We would be much better served knowing what our candidates stand for and expecting that they will stand for those very things in office, even if we don't always entirely agree with them.

Gay Marriage

It hardly seems possible that the fight over gay marriage would become such a pivotal battle in this Culture War, but it appears from all indications that gay marriage was "the straw that broke the camel's back" in the 2004 presidential election. The other primary issues of the Culture War—abortion, gun control and separation of church and state—have been significant political issues for more than 30 years while the gay marriage controversy is a relative newcomer. The escalation of the fight over gay marriage brought the Culture War into the public spotlight, transforming it from a minor skirmish into a full-blown conflict. As a stand-alone issue, gay marriage would not have had the kind of impact it eventually did have on the electoral process.

Hardly anyone predicted that heat from the gay marriage issue would ignite the firestorm of the Culture War. One commentator who did predict this outcome was Stanly Kurtz, a National Review Online contributing editor. In the National Review Online edition of November 26, 2002, he had this to say about the political firestorm that was about to be unleashed:

> This coming summer, the Massachusetts Supreme Judicial Court is likely to legalize gay marriage. If that happens, a convulsive national battle over gay marriage will break out—right in the middle of the next presidential-election season. The ultimate outcome of our coming national culture war over gay marriage will either be legal gay marriage throughout the United States, or passage of the Federal Marriage Amendment, which defines mar-

riage as the union of one man and one woman. There will be no middle ground.

So if gay marriage is legalized in Massachusetts this coming summer, several things will ensue. First, gay couples will flood into Massachusetts from across the country to get married. Returning to their home states, they will file a series of lawsuits at the state and federal levels seeking to compel recognition of the marriages performed in Massachusetts. The airwaves will be filled with tales of gay couples outraged by the fact that a simple drive across state lines invalidates their marriage.

All this will galvanize opponents of gay marriage. It will immediately become apparent that the extra-legislative decision of a few judges in Massachusetts threatens to impose gay marriage on the entire country.

Right now, hardly a politician in the country wants to talk about gay marriage. Liberals fear that favoring it will mark them as culturally radical. Conservatives fear that opposing it will label them as hard-hearted "homophobes." Like abortion, politicians dread the gay-marriage issue because it cannot be easily compromised.

The gay-marriage battle will accentuate the culturally based red/blue split in the electorate.

I have no idea if Mr. Kurtz's crystal ball is always this accurate, but in this case, he couldn't have been more prescient. His prediction was wrong in only one detail—the speed with which the Massachusetts Supreme Court would act. The court didn't wait until the summer of 2004 as predicted, but instead acted within days of this article, ruling in late November of 2003 that the state of Massachusetts could not ban gay couples from marrying. The firestorm was unleashed immediately. Efforts by the governor and state legislature to quickly circumvent the court decision were front page news, but were ultimately unsuccessful. It was soon concluded that the only way to reverse the decision was through an amendment to the state constitution. The process was started immediately, but the amendment process in Massachusetts is a painstakingly slow process. It will take until November 2006 to complete it. An appeal to the Supreme Court of the United States was filed, but the Supreme Court decided not to hear the appeal and offered no comment on why it wished to stay on the sidelines.

Thus same-sex marriage is now legal in Massachusetts and will remain so until at least November of 2006. Just as Kurtz predicted, gay couples from around the country have flocked to Massachusetts to get married. They return home to states that refuse to recognize their marriage. It won't be long before a multitude of court cases are underway challenging any state's right to refuse recognition of a Massachusetts marriage. The cases will slowly wind through the judicial system and undoubtedly end up in the Supreme Court. If the Court decides that every state must recognize legal marriages performed in any state, the door will be wide open for any gay couple to travel to Massachusetts and return home legally married. In essence, with the minor inconvenience of a trip to Massachusetts, gay marriage would be legal everywhere in the United States, in spite of existing state legislation to the contrary. As Kurtz points out, the only way to circumvent this probable eventuality is an amendment to the Constitution of the United States that bans same-sex marriage. President Bush campaigned openly for just such a constitutional amendment that would take the decision out of the courts and put it in the hands of the public. Conversely, the majority of legislators from both political parties believe there is adequate legal precedent to indicate that the Supreme Court will not overrule state law on the subject of marriage and are therefore unwilling to pursue a constitutional amendment. With the election now behind us, other national priorities, such as the ongoing war against terror and social security reform, have returned to the forefront as the same-sex marriage amendment discussion languishes in the background. We shouldn't be surprised when an adverse decision by an appeals court propels this to the forefront sometime within the next year.

Kurtz and others were able to predict the Massachusetts battle by following the trajectory of relevant cases as they moved through the courts, but no one could have predicted how one man in San Francisco would single-handedly turn this into a bicoastal firestorm. In February 2004, just as the presidential campaign was heating up, the mayor of San Francisco, Gavin Newsom, decided to take matters into his own hands and began issuing marriage licenses for gay partners. It was Newsome's own interpretation of the California State Constitution that led him to the conclusion that:

> "We are reading the direct language within the state constitution, and we directed our county clerk to do the right thing and extend the privilege that's extended to my wife and myself and millions of us across the country to same-sex couples," San Francisco Mayor Gavin Newsom told CNN in mid-February.

—Online NewsHour, April 30, 2004

Now, thanks to one judge in Massachusetts and one mayor in San Francisco, gay marriages were being performed on both coasts at the same time. It didn't help matters that both of these spectacles were near the media hubs of New York and Los Angeles. The three time zones that separated the two ring circus of gay marriage facilitated nearly round the clock coverage of the unfolding controversy. Activists on both sides of the issue made the most of it. Every cable news channel was filled with commentary and visual images of gay immigrants making their way to San Francisco and Massachusetts to take advantage of the opportunity, however short-lived it might be. Fortunately, San Francisco's time in the media spotlight was relatively short. Newsome's self-appointed tenure as chief judge of California ended March 11, 2004 when the California Supreme Court ordered San Francisco City Hall to stop issuing marriage licenses to same-sex couples. In the course of one month more than 4,000 marriage licenses had been issued.

The impact of these two spectacles on the 2004 election was immediate and significant. Though many Democrats spoke out strongly in opposition to gay marriage, there was enough sympathy and support from within the Democratic Party for the general public to conclude this issue was part of the Democratic agenda. Conversely, Republicans were nearly unanimous in opposition to gay marriage. Democratic candidates paid dearly for the perception that gay marriage was a plank in the party platform. A Gallup poll conducted in the summer of 2004 found the following:

> Do you think marriages between homosexuals should or should not be recognized by the law as valid, with the same rights as traditional marriages?

Should Be Valid	Should Not Be Valid	No Opinion
32%	62%	6%

An issue supported by only 32 percent of the public is not an issue that a candidate wants to be burdened with, and right or wrong, the perception was that Democrats supported gay marriage and Republicans opposed it. It's impossible to quantify the significance of this one issue to red voters, but it's almost a certainty that its addition to the already simmering frustration over abortion, gun control and church-state issues solidified support for Republican candidates and energized red voters to turn out in record numbers.

In another significant measure of the strength of the gay marriage opposition, 42 of the 50 states have implemented legislation or constitutional amendments to prevent gay marriage. These laws are not the result of opinion polls. The passage of these laws represents the will of real voters. The laws are typically called defense of marriage acts, or DOMAs. Even more telling is the fact that 13 states scrambled to place constitutional amendments banning gay marriage on the 2004 ballot. All 13 passed by overwhelming majorities:

- Alabama   (86%)

- Arkansas   (76%)

- Georgia   (76%)

- Kentucky   (75%)
- Louisiana   (78%)
- Michigan   (59%)
- Missouri   (71%)
- Montana   (66%)
- North Dakota   (73%)
- Ohio   (62%)
- Oklahoma   (76%)
- Oregon   (57%)
- Utah   (66%)

Can there be any doubt that red voters were energized and moti-vated to show up at the polls on election day to ensure that gay mar-riage was defeated? Many political commentators were caught off guard with the magnitude of the turnout. Long lines of persistent vot-ers were commonplace. Nationwide, participation of eligible voters exceeded 60 percent, which is the strongest level of participation since the bitter election of 1968.

In retrospect, it seems quite predictable when viewed in the light of public opposition to gay marriage and the opportunity for voters to register that sentiment at the ballot box. Ten of the states on this list were safely red, but turnout was much greater than anticipated as vot-ers flocked to the polls to shoot down gay marriage. This unantici-pated turnout in safe states certainly helped President Bush increase his national vote margin. More importantly, from an electoral stand-point, three key swing states were on this list, states that could have gone either way in the election—Missouri, Michigan and Ohio. Bush won two of the three. In particular, Ohio turned out to be the state that determined the winner. Had Bush lost Ohio, John Kerry would be president today. Bush managed to get 51 percent of the vote in Ohio—a state that voted down gay marriage by 62 percent. Rural and suburban Ohioans came out in record numbers, likely as a direct result of the gay marriage ballot question. These rural and suburban voters favored Bush over Kerry by a significant margin. Bush clearly benefited not only from the stand he took on gay marriage, but more importantly, from the lift in conservative voter turnout the issue generated. It's quite possible, if not downright likely, that Bush would have lost the election if banning gay marriage had not been on the ballot in Ohio. Not only was gay marriage the "last straw" in the Culture War, it is very likely the "straw" that broke John Kerry's electoral back. Isn't it ironic that gay activists, pushing a gay agenda in an election year, likely caused the defeat of the presidential candidate most supportive of their cause? And at the same time it unleashed a backlash from a public that until this point has generally been sympathetic to the gay rights agenda. It's a stunning reminder of the law of unintended consequences.

Pandora's Box

It may have seemed like the gay marriage issue came out of nowhere to take a prominent place in the Culture War last year, but gay marriage has been the subject of a mostly under-the-radar battle for much of the past decade. My own first encounter with the issue was in California in the weeks leading up to the 2000 election. An initiative was on the California ballot that would define marriage to be "between a man and a woman only." Friends asked if I would participate in a grass roots effort to knock on doors in our neighborhood and determine whether each household was "for" or "against" the proposition. If the household was in favor of the initiative, I was to record the voter's name and phone number and call them the day of the election to remind them to vote. I readily admit that I was extremely reluctant to participate, not only because it would be several painful hours doing something I would not enjoy at all, but primarily because I didn't feel strongly one way or the other about gay marriage. If anything, I was more sympathetic than antagonistic toward gay marriage. I, like most Americans, really don't care what goes on in private between two adults. I didn't see how gay marriage would cause any public harm. The request for me to get involved caused me to undergo some significant soul-searching. After careful consideration, I gradually came to believe that state sanction of same-sex marriage was not a good idea. I willingly participated in the effort to ban same-sex marriage in California and am glad it was successful.

In my own soul-searching on this issue, I was reminded of the ancient Greek myth of Pandora and her infamous box. In the myth,

Pandora was the first mortal female created by the gods of Mount Olympus. She entered a mortal world of perfect innocence and content. Evils such as hunger, cold, sickness and death did not exist. Pandora was beautiful, and Epimetheus, one of the previously created males, couldn't resist her attractiveness. Together they lived an idyllic life, until one day the god Mercury stopped by their home and asked if he could leave a burdensome box with them. He was tired of carrying the box and hoped to rid himself of the burden as he continued on to his destination. He would recover the box when he passed that way again. Pandora and Epimetheus consented to keep the box for Mercury. As soon as Mercury was on his way, Pandora developed a strong desire to open the box and view its contents. Epimetheus advised against the invasion of private property, but he soon departed, leaving Pandora alone with the box. She began to hear whisperings from the box. The mysterious contents were pleading with her saying, "Pandora, have pity on us and free us from this prison." Now even more curious about the contents of the box, she complied with the request. As soon as the lid was lifted, a multitude of insects escaped from the box. In the myth, each insect represented a different mortal ill—hunger, fear, cold, illness and a host of other difficulties—that would now begin to afflict the previously perfect world of mortality. It took a while, but eventually the ills of this one little box of insects infected the entire mortal world.

Like the pleas Pandora heard coming from within the box, the pleas of the gay community for our acceptance of gay marriage are not easy to ignore. They appeal to our sense of fairness and our respect for free choice. Why not allow gay couples the same rights as heterosexual couples? Isn't it a fundamental American principle that all men and women, regardless of race, gender, sexual orientation, or any other personal attributes, are entitled to equal treatment under the law? Of course that's true. But I came to realize that supporting individual gay rights while at the same time rejecting gay marriage was not incompatible with these principles. Furthermore, I came to realize that governmental sanction of same-sex marriage would be like opening

Pandora's Box, unleashing both legal and cultural influences that would be very detrimental to our society in the long run.

Let's first consider the legal implications. Today, marriage law in the United States is not a federal responsibility. The legal definition of marriage, divorce and anything else pertaining to marriage is entirely determined by each individual state. Each state can have different practices—that's why certain states are considered more convenient for marriage and divorce than others. In fact, couples often travel across state lines to take advantage of slight differences in marriage law to suit their particular situation. However, with the recent exception of Massachusetts, all states have one thing in common: Marriage is between one man and one woman only.

There is nothing in the United States Constitution concerning marriage and there is only one federal law concerning marriage, the Defense of Marriage Act (DOMA) which was implemented by Congress and President Clinton in 1992. This law actually works against gay marriage, stipulating that any state that has implemented its own defense of marriage act—limiting marriage to a man and a woman—is not required to recognize same-sex marriages performed in other states. In other words, Ohio, or any other state with a DOMA law, doesn't have to recognize a same-sex marriage performed in Massachusetts.

It doesn't take a law degree to understand what would happen if the Supreme Court eventually declares any state DOMA law unconstitutional. State legislatures and state courts would no longer have the ability to determine who participates in marriage. It would be like Roe v. Wade all over again. A handful of justices would overturn the expressed will of the people, which is overwhelmingly against same-sex marriage. Worse than that, it would open the door for unions of one man and several women, one woman and several men, several men and several women, or any other combination of marriage partners you can dream up. One of these potential configurations is already well known to us as polygamy. We are aware of polygamy because a considerable number of Americans participate in such illegal unions today. You can well imagine that if the Supreme Court strikes down state DOMA laws, it wouldn't be long before the justice system would be flooded with legal action to overturn restrictions on polygamy, polyandry and a host of other odd-ball unions that we can't even conceive of presently.

The frightening thing is that this flurry of legal activity would certainly be successful. The courts couldn't say on the one hand that marriage between one man and one woman is discrimination against gays and on the other hand say that it is completely acceptable to discriminate against those who believe in polygamy, polyandry, or any other concept of marriage. The court would have to adopt the legal principle of equal rights for all, not special rights for some. The only way to prevent the complete collapse of our nation's ability to define marriage would be for the states to construct a law that specified marriage was between one man and one woman, or between one man and one man, or between one woman and one woman. This approach would never succeed on three counts. First, no legislative body in the country, either state or federal, would approve such a law in the face of massive public opposition, as evidenced in the poll cited in the previous chapter. Second, if the Supreme Court attempted to impose such a construction, the court would be making law, not interpreting it. At this point, I know you are thinking that the Supreme Court has overstepped its bounds before, why wouldn't it on this issue? When the court has gone beyond interpretation and lapsed into legislation, it has had at least some marginal legal excuse. In this particular case, there wouldn't even be the most marginal of justification. Absolutely no legal precedent or justification exists to support such a conclusion. Third, a law written this specifically would grant special rights to two groups of Americans—same-sex couples and couples participating in traditional one man, one woman marriages. The only grounds on which the court could have rejected traditional marriage in the first place is on the basis that it provides special rights to men and women who believe in traditional marriage. It would be completely illogical to then create a new law that extends the same special rights to gays, but excludes all others. The inconsistency of such a circular argument is too obvious for any court to approve.

Over time, we would most certainly end up with marriages of all types. This country—along with nearly every other country in the world—has long resisted any departure from traditional marriage, and the resistance is not just for the sake of maintaining an age-old tradition or of conforming to religious practice. Nearly all societies throughout recorded history have recognized the need for the social—not necessarily religious—institution of marriage. Societies promote marriage for three primary reasons: 1) perpetuation of the society; 2) development and support of children; and 3) as a structure to maintain personal property rights. Nearly every society that has ever existed has reached the conclusion that monogamy between one man and one woman is the form of marriage that best suits the three objectives of marriage. Certainly there have been exceptions, but even anthropologists studying the earliest evidence of societal behavior have concluded that monogamous relationships between one man and one woman are predominant. Many who support same-sex marriage look upon current marriage law as the imposition of somebody else's religious practice upon them. In short, they consider it a form of state-mandated religious practice and consider it a violation of the First Amendment. It's true that state and religious observance of marriage are often one and the same, but it is also true that nearly all societies throughout recorded history have recognized the need for a social institution of marriage, regardless of religious practice. If the influence of religion did not exist, we would still have arrived at precisely the same definition of marriage. Any appeal to the First Amendment is a red herring.

It shouldn't be surprising that virtually all societies would reach a similar conclusion concerning monogamy when the primary concerns of civil society are considered. Society is not unlike any living, breathing organism in the sense that it seeks self-preservation. It shouldn't be surprising that a society would encourage men and women to join together to reproduce and restock the society. Likewise, it shouldn't be surprising that a society encourages men and women to stay together as husband and wife in order to raise the children produced by their union. It's the most logical way to ensure the proper development of children. If it were common practice for either parent to abandon his or her offspring, how would children develop into productive members of society? The society would either exist in chaos or would need to develop other structures for raising children. It would be a logistical nightmare to put in place an alternative system. I know you are thinking that we have already succumbed to that problem in America today with a runaway divorce rate and a heartbreaking level of single-parenthood. But imagine how bad it would be if there were absolutely no marriage laws in place. It's bad enough now with reasonably strong marriage laws and considerable social pressure on delinquent parents to shape-up. But can you imagine the federal day-care and night-care system that would be required if the traditional family no longer existed? It would not only be logistically complex, it could not possibly be as effective as a properly functioning traditional marriage in raising children.

Though property rights sounds like a very mundane concern to associate with marriage, its importance should not be minimized. All societies need rules for the acquisition, ownership and disposition of private properties of all types. Inheritance of personal property is more easily managed within the framework of a traditional family than in any other relationship structure. You can imagine the difficulty of determining ownership of property in a promiscuous, polygamist or for that matter, any non-monogamous society. Either property would be inherited according to the laws of the jungle—every man, woman and child for themselves—or the inheritance laws would be exceptionally complex.

Marriage between one man and one woman is without doubt the most important fundamental building block of our society. In fact, those few societies without traditional marriage inevitably evolve toward it, not away from it. Advocates of nontraditional marriage are quick to point out that the institution of traditional marriage is already waning, falling victim to single-parenthood and serial divorce. They should be more careful in selecting their evidence. The observable detrimental outcomes of single-parenthood and a high divorce rate are the best evidence for encouraging and strengthening traditional marriage and, therefore, the best arguments against further erosion of marriage through the legalization of same-sex unions. Nobody likes to talk openly about this, but everyone knows that single-parenthood and high divorce rates are primary contributors to the obvious deterioration of American culture in recent years. There are of course exceptions, where one parent is unfit to be either spouse or parent. In these rare cases, single-parenthood is a better alternative than a dysfunctional traditional family. But let's not mistake the exception for the rule. In the vast majority of cases, it's not parental inadequacy, but parental selfishness that leads to divorce and single-parenthood. Most often, divorce occurs when couples with children allow personal goals, aspirations and desires to take precedence over what is best for the children.

And obviously it isn't just divorce that is increasing the ranks of single-parenthood. The number of unwed mothers has skyrocketed in the past 40 years. There are a whole host of reasons for this trend, a discussion of which would fill an entire book on its own. I feel confident that if such a book were written, the bottom line conclusion would be that our society has encouraged promiscuity by promoting and glamorizing sex as a personal pleasure to be enjoyed as often as possible; and at the same time, society has discouraged any moral teaching to the contrary, topping it off by absolving participants of personal accountability for the inevitable harmful outcomes of sexual promiscuity. It's a mouthful when expressed as one lengthy sentence, but I think it would be disingenuous for anyone to disagree with the three premises contained in the sentence:

- Sex is promoted in the mass media as a pleasurable end, in and of itself, that everyone is entitled to enjoy frequently, married or not.

- Moral beliefs to the contrary, whether religious or secular, are made light of as old fashioned and unrealistic.

- When a woman gets pregnant, neither participant is held accountable.

As recent evidence of the acceleration and detrimental impact of these three trends, consider the following excerpts from three news articles, each appearing separately in late 2005. First, on the promotion of sex by the mass media:

> More than a year after federal authorities launched a crackdown on broadcast indecency, television remains so awash in sex that 7 in 10 episodes include some kind of racy content, a study released Wednesday shows. The results from the Henry J. Kaiser Family Foundation also found that the number of sexual scenes in sitcoms, dramas and reality shows nearly doubled since 1998, while depictions of abstinence or "safe sex" were on the wane.

> Kaiser, a nonprofit group in Menlo Park, Calif., makes no recommendations in its report. But Kaiser officials said they hoped it would focus attention on whether television influenced casual attitudes toward sex by teens, who the study estimates watch 20 hours of TV a week." We are not saying TV is to blame for this phenomenon," said University of Arizona communications professor Dale Kunkel, who helped conduct the study. "But research is indicating that TV has an impact."

> Still, Tony Perkins, president of the Washington-based Family Research Council, said the Kaiser study underscored the belief among many parents that television was having a coarsening effect on their kids. "It's not the same today as when I was growing up and parents left their kids in front of the TV to watch 'Captain Kangaroo,'" Perkins said. "The sex depicted on television does have an effect on kids. If we are what we eat, then we become what we watch."

—Jube Shiver Jr., Los Angeles Times Staff Writer, November 10, 2005

Second, evidence of the ridicule, erosion and even collapse of traditional moral values concerning sexuality:

Freewheeling young women in the United States and Canada first have intercourse at the age of 15, partake more in oral sex than previous generations and are far less prudish, according to a landmark new report by researchers at California's San Diego State University.

"Feelings of sexual guilt plummeted, especially among young women. Attitudes toward premarital sex became dramatically more liberal over the same period," the analysis of 530 studies spanning five decades and involving more than a quarter of a million young people said.

Over the same 56-year period, approval of premarital sex increased from 12 percent to 73 percent among young women, while the figure rose from 40 percent to 79 percent among young men, according to the study.

"The change in young women's beliefs about premarital sex was enormous," said Jean Twenge, a psychology professor at San Diego State University who co-authored the report with Brooke Wells of City University of New York.

The study revealed that the massive cultural revolution that swept North America in the past 30 years had contributed dramatically to the shift as movies and television shows tackled formerly taboo topics such as teenage pregnancy, abortion, sexually transmitted diseases and rape.

—Young Women Lead the Way in Tearing Down Sex Taboos: New US Survey, Brietbart.com, October 4, 2005

And finally, evidence of one of the many undesirable outcomes, a dramatic increase in the number of unmarried mothers:

> Nearly 1.5 million babies, a record, were born to unmarried women in the United Sates last year, the government reported on Friday. And it isn't just teenagers any more. "People have the impression that teens and unmarried mothers are synonymous," said Stephanie Ventura of the National Center for Health Statistics.
>
> The increase in unmarried births have been among women in their 20s, she said, particularly those 25 to 29.
>
> Among teens, more than 80 percent of mothers were unmarried.
>
> —Randolph E. Schmid, Associated Press, October 28, 2005

As a society, we ought to be ashamed. We have sown the wind and are now reaping the whirlwind. An entire array of empirical evidence could be submitted to make the case that single-parenthood is having a negative impact on our society. But instead, I'll simply ask you to reflect on your personal answer to this question, "Is there any doubt in your mind that, with very few exceptions, a traditional family is the best environment for the development of children?" I'm confident that you, along with nearly every other American, will agree with the proposition that a traditional family is the best possible structure for the development of children. As a society we ought to do everything possible to encourage traditional marriage and avoid anything that discourages or destroys it.

This leads me back to the topic at hand—same-sex marriage. It might seem odd that I have spent such considerable energy discussing single-parent families in the context of a debate concerning gay marriage. Especially since many, if not most, same-sex marriages would produce no children to worry about anyway. How could a childless same-sex marriage be detrimental to society? The simple answer is that same-sex marriage is detrimental because it dilutes the value of traditional marriage in the eyes of the public. If there are additional alternatives to traditional marriage, there will be less emphasis on the importance of traditional marriage. With the addition of another alternative, it will be diluted even more than it has already been diluted by the alternatives of divorce and single-parenthood. The argument that "we shouldn't worry about adding gay marriage to the laundry list of problems already afflicting traditional marriage because traditional marriage is already screwed-up" is dead wrong. Doesn't adding gasoline to a fire make it worse? We should spend more time devising ways to strengthen and encourage traditional marriage, not finding more ways to destroy it. If the vast majority of us agree that erosion of traditional marriage has been detrimental to society, why in the world would we seek to further dilute it? It would be a giant step in the wrong direction.

Additionally, gay parenthood is becoming increasingly popular, and there isn't any doubt that same-sex marriage would accelerate that trend. How could it be otherwise? It's inevitable that gay couples would be more bold and confident about child rearing if the couples are in a state-sanctioned marriage. State sanction ensures it would not only be legally acceptable, but over time, it would become culturally acceptable for gay couples to raise children. We all know that gay parents love their children as much as heterosexual parents love theirs. In fact, I readily admit that there are far more derelict heterosexual parents than derelict gay parents. Gay parents who are making the effort to raise a child in spite of all the obstacles they will encounter are likely more committed to child development than most heterosexual parents. But we have to face the reality that children of gay parents will face challenges that would not have existed had they been children of parents in a traditional marriage. Growing up is hard enough under ideal circumstances. It is significantly more difficult in a non-traditional family structure. Why make life harder on a child than it needs to be? I understand the desire of gay parents to have and raise children. It is the most challenging and rewarding undertaking in life. I wouldn't try to prevent or even discourage gay couples from adopting or raising their own children. I understand and appreciate the noble desire and recognize that children of such unions are most often grateful offspring and wonderful people. But I certainly wouldn't encourage or promote it, which is exactly what will occur if same-sex marriage is legalized.

Preserving and promoting traditional marriage—between one man and one woman—is a good idea that has been validated by history. It isn't just an American value, but a value recognized by nearly every civil society from time immemorial. Don't be confused by those who would claim it is purely a religious institution. Traditional marriage is the basic building block of civil society. It provides for the perpetuation of the society and the development of the future citizens of that society. It's such a "good idea" that nearly every country in the world has practiced it forever. Anything we do that dilutes traditional marriage, including easy divorce, promiscuity, and yes, same-sex marriage, will undoubtedly have a negative impact on society. These detrimental effects will be greatly magnified by the variety of other nontraditional marriages that would be spawned by any legal decision in favor of same-sex marriage. We should be very careful with the building blocks of society. Once weakened and deteriorating, they are almost impossible to restore to their former strength. Opening the lid of Pandora's nontraditional marriage box will unleash long-term forces that would be clearly detrimental to American society.

Enough Already

I have heard several versions of a story about an overzealous salesman. They all go something like this:

> Fred, an ambitious but inexperienced car salesman, is working with a potential customer, Mary. Mary knows exactly how much she can afford to spend on a new car, and she is neither willing nor able to spend one penny more. She has found a car on Fred's lot with the features and sticker price that meet her needs and is now working with Fred to finalize the sale. In her mind, the decision is made, the sale, complete. All that remains is the paperwork. In Fred's mind, the sale has just begun. While beginning the paperwork, he asks Mary if she would like the optional leather seats in her new car. Mary, knowing they will cost more, says no. Fred persists, educating Mary about the enhanced comfort and long-term value of the leather seats. Mary resists. Eventually, Fred gives up on the seat upgrade and proceeds to offer Mary the optional stereo package. Mary again says no. She has a budget to keep. Fred again persists. And so it goes for quite some time, option after option after option. Eventually, a frustrated Mary declares she is no longer interested in any purchase and leaves without purchasing the car.

The moral of the story is obvious. A successful salesman listens to the customer and understands how much, if any, "selling" is appropriate with that particular customer. If a salesman continues to sell beyond the customer's willingness to be sold, the customer is likely to say "enough already," and the sale is lost entirely.

That's kind of how I feel about the gay agenda. I am 100 percent in support of the efforts of the gay community to ensure their civil rights are protected and that gays are treated with dignity and respect. I unequivocally support any effort to ensure that individual choice of private lifestyle is not only legally protected, but also culturally respected. I, like most Americans, really don't care what consenting adults do in private, and I certainly don't want anyone to face discrimination in public because of their lifestyle. Through difficult and persistent effort, activists in the gay community have been extremely successful at ensuring civil rights protection for all gays. And through education, persuasion and perseverance they have significantly reduced the cultural stigma long associated with being gay. The transformation is startling when compared to the way things were when I was much younger. Incidents of verbal abuse, disrespect, hostility and even malicious treatment were commonplace. I don't remember anyone, adult or child, who showed any consideration or respect for gay people. I do remember plenty of disrespect and downright meanness directed at gays. In the rural community I lived in, any gay person was treated as a total outcast. Any public mention of gays brought derisive and undignified comments. It's hard to believe how much society's attitude toward gays has changed in the past 40 years. Yes, there are still too many anti-gay bigots in America. But I think an unbiased observer would be compelled by the facts to conclude that the progress made has been remarkable, given how bad it was back then. The evidence of this transformation is all around us. There are many celebrities who are openly gay. There are a good number of TV shows and movies featuring gay actors and even a few featuring gay lifestyles. Most of us have friends and neighbors who are openly gay. Such openness was not possible 40 years ago. There is no doubt in my mind that we are a better society as a result of these changes. They were necessary to ensure that all Americans—regardless of race, creed or sexual preference—are treated with respect and given the same rights as anyone else. I'm all for continued progress on any front where it is necessary to remove the vestiges of discrimination and disrespect.

But when it comes to gay marriage, I have to say "enough already." I don't believe that saying "no" to same-sex marriage is at all inconsistent with saying "yes" to civil rights for gays. Marriage is not an individual civil right. It's a social structure implemented by government for the good of society in general. And in this society, as in most others throughout history, an overwhelming majority of citizens has concluded that our society is best served by a very specific legal definition of marriage: the union of one man and one woman. It's not a denial of civil rights to deny a person the opportunity to participate in marriage. We have established thousands of laws, rules and regulations restricting participation in all sorts of activities. For example, if you are under 16 years of age, you are not eligible for a driver's license. If you are under 35 years of age, you are not eligible to be president of the United States. If your grades aren't good enough, you won't be admitted to state college. If you don't have $20 you are willing to part with, you won't be admitted to a national park. I'm sure you can continue this list in your own mind for a long time, but I hope the point is already made. These restrictions exist because collectively we have decided that our society is better off with some form of exclusion in each of these activities. Marriage is just one in a long list of activities with such restrictions on participation. You can imagine the chaos that would develop if government had no ability or right to restrict participation in anything. Government not only has the right, it also has the obligation to ensure that such restrictions are in place for the protection and "good order" of society.

I know I am not the only one who feels this way. Most Americans are glad that gays are winning the battles for civil rights and public respect. The cultural changes we have witnessed in the last 40 years are sufficient proof of that. These changes would not have happened

without significant public support. The Gallup poll I referenced earlier confirms it:

Do you think it should be legal or should not be legal for two
men who are consenting adults to have sex with each other in
their own home?

Should Be Legal	Should Not Be Legal	No Opinion
62%	31%	7%

Do you think it should be legal or should not be legal for two
women who are consenting adults to have sex with each other in
their own home?

Should Be Legal	Should Not Be Legal	No Opinion
63%	30%	7%

As you may know, there has been considerable discussion in the
news regarding the rights of homosexual men and women. In
general do you think homosexuals should or should not have
equal rights in terms of job opportunities?

Yes Should	No Should Not	Depends/No Opinion
89%	8%	3%

Do you favor or oppose allowing openly gay men and lesbian
women to serve in the military?

Favor	Oppose	No Opinion
63%	32%	5%

The high level of public support for civil rights protection and cultural acceptance for gays expressed in this poll is truly remarkable given our recent past. But in this very same poll, when asked

> Do you think marriages between homosexuals should or should not be recognized by the law as valid, with the same rights as traditional marriages?

Should Be Valid	Should Not Be Valid	No Opinion
32%	62%	6%

I don't think there could be any clearer indication that the general public is saying "enough already." The American public has been, and will continue to be, supportive of civil rights protection and cultural acceptance for gays. But Americans recognize—for all of the reasons I have indicated—that the institution of marriage should be restricted to one man and one woman.

Disarming

If the premise of this book is true—that a majority of Americans are in favor of banning abortion on demand and gay marriage, strengthening gun controls and supporting separation of church and state—what, if anything, can be done to advance this agenda? Unfortunately, the two major parties in our two-party political system don't offer this agenda as an option. So when it comes time to vote anyone who supports this alternative has to choose which of the cultural issues are more important to them. We can vote Republican and be well represented on the issues of abortion and gay marriage. Or we can vote Democratic and be well represented on the issues of gun control and separation of church and state. We occasionally have the opportunity to vote for a "maverick," someone who differs with the party-line on these issues, but for the most part our political menu is not ala carte. No matter which party we choose a significant portion of the selection will be distasteful to us.

I'm not complaining. I believe the two-party system generally serves us quite well. The positives far outweigh the negatives. It's hard enough for two political parties to negotiate the compromises necessary for our system of government to work. If there were three or more political parties, each with substantial support, you could well imagine how difficult it would be to govern. No single party would constitute a majority. Nothing would get done without a three sided compromise. It's difficult to get constructive compromise from two parties. It would be nearly impossible with three or more. Government would either be in perpetual gridlock or reach watered-down compromises that wouldn't be satisfying to anyone.

However, in spite of the obvious virtues of the two-party system, the Culture War greatly magnifies one of its downsides. In the not too distant past, both major political parties were more flexible than they are presently, allowing—even encouraging—members to take positions not entirely in line with party platforms. Even if a candidate didn't agree with every party position, there was still a reasonable chance he or she could end up as the party's candidate for office. For example, just a couple of decades ago it wasn't unusual to see Republican candidates who were pro-abortion and Democratic candidates who were anti-abortion, even though their positions ran counter to their respective party platforms. Unfortunately, this is no longer the case. Now both parties are so entrenched in this Culture War, it's nearly impossible for a candidate to get nominated for office if he or she is not in lock-step with the party line.

Why the change? Why have the two political parties moved away from accepting diversity of thought to requiring that their candidates pass a "litmus test" on these cultural issues? There are many contributing factors, but the factor most relevant to this discussion is the willingness of the silent majority to just stand by and let it happen. Both parties have roughly 40 percent of the electorate in full agreement with their respective party platform. The 20 percent of voters who are not in full agreement with either party platform—the silent majority—have been ambivalent on these cultural issues. The silent majority simply has been uninterested and unwilling to take a strong stand against what the parties offer. As long as the silent majority acquiesces to the current party platforms, there will be no incentive for the parties to change.

Several things can and ought to be done to pressure both political parties to either revise their platforms entirely or, at a minimum, give dissenting party members a chance to become candidates for office. The first, and most obvious, is that we should vote for candidates who support this agenda. Many people in both parties agree with these positions in spite of their party platforms. Over time, if a meaningful number of these candidates are elected, party positions will change. After all, political parties are in the business of winning elections and will follow the votes. Unfortunately, though I wholeheartedly support this type of effort—and we absolutely need to pursue it—it's not likely to make much difference anytime soon. In the current political climate, it's almost impossible for a candidate who does not toe the party line to get his or her name on a ballot. The party selection process is heavily weighted in favor of party loyalists who currently have more than enough strength to force the status quo on the party. Mavericks will seldom get the opportunity to run. So, though we have a long-term need and an obligation to work through the parties, change, if it comes at all, will be painfully slow.

Given the difficulty of changing the two major parties, forming a third party might seem like an attractive solution. But the history of third parties is a discouraging reminder that this tactic is not likely to work. We can look to very recent political history for insight into the viability of a third party. The Reform Party created by Ross Perot and his followers in 1992 was the most successful ever in a presidential election. Perot won the support of nearly 20 percent of the national electorate that year. Though he was not elected, Perot's party did have a significant impact on the election, and for the remainder of the decade it continued to have a significant influence on both major parties. Both parties recognized that Perot voters were discontent with the status quo. Not surprisingly, in an effort to win back Perot voters, both parties incorporated elements of Perot's political philosophy in their own platforms. The Republican sponsored "Contract with America," introduced for the mid-term elections of 1994, was taken almost entirely from Perot's campaign themes. Not surprisingly, it helped Republicans gain seats in both houses of Congress that year. Likewise, in 1996, the Democrats converted to Perot's gospel of balanced budgets after a lengthy history of budget busting and deficit creation.

It's clear that Perot's third party option significantly influenced the two major parties. So why not go that route again? I don't think the success of Perot's third party bid is likely to be repeated any time soon. The hurdles faced by any third party are almost insurmountable. I'm sure Perot would agree. The first hurdle is funding. How do you raise the hundreds of millions of dollars required to compete against the two major parties? I don't think it can be done unless a candidate is willing to spend many millions of their own fortune on the effort. Perot had the financial resources and the willingness to spend it, but that club has a very limited membership. The second hurdle is that the two major parties are incredibly adept at squashing any competition. When they are engaged in a battle for survival, they will go to great lengths to come out on top, and it isn't a pleasant experience for the third party or its candidate. If you have any doubts about how tough and dirty it can get, just ask Perot what he, his family and supporters endured as political operatives of both parties set their sights on destroying the Reform Party. The final hurdle is that the third party can actually cause detrimental, unintended effects. In 1992, Perot siphoned away 20 percent of the vote, allowing Bill Clinton to be elected president with only a 42 percent plurality—far short of a majority. It's difficult for a president to get anything done with less than 50 percent support. It's also quite possible that Clinton wouldn't even have been elected president had Perot not been on the ballot. There are many who believe Perot voters had more in common with Bush voters than with Clinton voters and would have gravitated to President Bush in the absence of Perot. If that's true—and I tend to think it is—the unintended consequence was the election of the candidate with the least desirable agenda.

Besides these three hurdles, the long term benefits of a third party are questionable. Even though Republicans and Democrats co-opted most of Perot's agenda, the new-found religion was short-lived. Congress delivered balanced budgets for a couple of years but soon returned to deficit spending again. Overall, I think Perot's efforts were very good for the country, and I'm glad he did it. I just don't think it's likely to be repeated. I think the dramatic and unpredictable end of the Cold War, coupled with the inability of either party to recognize the simmering domestic issues that subsequently rocketed to the forefront, opened the door to a once-in-a-generation opportunity for Perot. He was in the right place at the right time. He had the right message and the financial resources to "take on" the system. I don't think that combination of pre-requisites is in place today, nor will it be anytime soon.

If a third party "end run" around the two major parties is unlikely, what can be done? I think a combination of working within the parties and around them in so-called "grass roots politics" can make substantial progress. We can find both Republican and Democratic candidates who support this agenda and are willing to buck the party line. But they need our participation and our votes to succeed. It requires members of the silent majority to end the silence and get involved in the primary election process. If we don't participate in sufficient numbers, we'll have nobody to blame but ourselves. In addition to supporting like-minded primary candidates, it would be even more effective for many of us take it one step further and become "activists" within the parties. It would be difficult for a party to ignore platform change if there was sufficient internal opposition to current platforms.

I think this "infiltration" of the parties is necessary, but not sufficient. It is a process that will bear fruit over time. However, the progress can be accelerated if we supplement party participation with non-partisan pressure from the outside. Nothing new needs to be created for this to work. There are many advocacy groups already in place on each of these Culture War issues. It's simply a matter of choosing the most appropriate organizations and getting involved. With increased participation and greater financial support, these advocacy groups could have a significant impact on our electoral process. Votes and money are the lifeblood of the political process, and these organizations could supply both if they are more broadly supported. The grass-roots battles over each of these cultural issues are currently a "draw" in terms of money and votes. As long as neither side has an advantage, there is no incentive for a shift in the status quo. A significant influx of resources to one side or the other would have tremendous impact on both parties. They would have no choice but to chase the money and votes to remain competitive. Significantly increasing support of the advocacy groups for these issues is the fastest and most powerful way to make a difference.

Whether within a political party, or in grass-roots advocacy groups, what specifically should we promote? I think each of the four issues of the Culture War requires a different approach. With abortion, I am absolutely convinced that a constitutional amendment should be pursued and enacted. I don't believe we should wait around for the appointment of new Supreme Court justices who might overturn Roe v. Wade. I know there is considerable hope that President Bush will have the opportunity in the next four years to appoint several Supreme Court justices, and the newly constituted Court will be conservative enough to overthrow Roe v. Wade. It's certainly true that Bush will have multiple opportunities to change the composition of the Court. He has already succeeded with the nomination of Chief Justice John Roberts and the nomination of Samuel Alito will be considered by the Senate in January, 2006. But who knows how any new member of the Court might vote on upcoming cases concerning abortion? Justices O'Conner and Kennedy were appointed by Ronald Reagan but have not delivered any significant blow to Roe v. Wade. Likewise with Justice Souter who was appointed by President Bush's father. Why should we believe that Roberts and Alito, or for that matter any future Bush appointment, will be any different? It seems that once on the Supreme Court any anti-abortion sentiment previously held by a justice is trumped by a concern for maintaining legal precedent. And the current form of approval process applied to Supreme Court nominees by the Senate Judiciary Committee almost ensures this will be the outcome. Candidates are grilled endlessly concerning their views with respect to observing legal precedent, and very specifically, their willingness to uphold Roe v. Wade. Once having gone on record with the Senate, and indirectly the entire nation, that Roe v. Wade is "settled law" it must be extremely difficult for a justice to not behave accordingly on future abortion cases. It's a very effective tactic by pro-abortion forces because it plays on two issues of primary importance to a jurist—the ability to decide cases only on the law in spite of contrary personal morality, and the desire to maintain the highest levels of personal integrity. Democrats accuse Republicans of having an abortion "litmus test" for judges, meaning Republicans will only accept judges who are against abortion. This has to be one of the most egregious examples of "the kettle calling the pot black" in the history of mankind. Democrats—in cooperation with a handful of Republicans—are dedicated to ensuring that nobody is appointed to the Supreme Court who won't uphold Roe v. Wade. I guess hypocrisy doesn't apply to Democratic litmus tests. It's a certainty that any judge who has expressed a contrary opinion—or even a willingness to contemplate one—will either not get nominated because of the certain political fight that will follow, or will be denied a confirmation vote through a filibuster by pro-abortion senators. The Republican majority currently has the ability to break a filibuster by changing the rules of the Senate—the so-called "nuclear option"—and we may well see that option exercised in January 2006 in order to place Alito on the Court. But even if Justices Roberts and Alito voted to overturn Roe v. Wade—and I've already pointed out that it's a "big if"—the court is still one vote short of overturning the decision. In any abortion case that comes before the Court, Roe will be reaffirmed by a 5 to 4 vote. The outcome will add one more precedent to Senator Specter's "super-duper precedent" chart and the next nominee will have an even bigger hill to climb. Or maybe not. If President Bush and the Republican Party continue the downhill slide in approval ratings triggered in late 2005 by the ongoing debate over Iraq and questionable Republican ethics, the next appointee could be facing a Democratic majority in the Senate instead of the current Republican majority. The nuclear option would then reappear as the "nuclear boomerang," enabling Democrats to ensure that the next justice—the justice who will hold the one vote that will decide the fate of Roe v. Wade—will be pro-abortion. Republicans will be taking a big risk if they decide to drop the nuclear-option bomb.

Even if Bush has the opportunity to appoint several conservative justices who then overturn Roe v. Wade, the decision will have no permanence. In the future, it's very likely that a more liberal president will have the opportunity to change the balance of the Court again, allowing a new group of justices to rule in favor of abortion. As I mentioned earlier, the Constitution is ambiguous about abortion and any representative group of justices is likely to come up with a split decision. I think we should remove all doubt and take the decision entirely out of the hands of judges. The only way to do this is to amend the Constitution in a way that recognizes the fetus as a human being. This will ensure that every fetus will be afforded the same right to life as any other person. A constitutional amendment not only takes this critical decision out of the hands of judges, but it also reaffirms our nation's commitment to human rights. It would be a complimentary and welcome addition to our founding principles, reaffirming the willingness of America to boldly defend the inalienable rights of all mankind.

I realize that previous attempts to amend the Constitution to prevent abortion have failed. Why would this time be any different? I think there are two primary reasons to be hopeful that a pro-life amendment would succeed this time around. First, the recently elevated political and social importance of these cultural issues is causing people to think more deeply about all of them. Over the years, these issues came at us independently. When taken in isolation, no single issue seemed large enough to worry about. Now, as we view them collectively, the potential negative social impact is more apparent. Secondly, the long term effects of Roe v. Wade—a decision made more than 30 years ago—are now plainly visible for all to see. Many of the social ills that opponents of abortion have predicted over the years have turned out to be true. I think many people felt that abortion would be rare, and, therefore, they just decided to go along with it on the basis that its effects would not be significant or widespread. The attitude was, "Why go through all the effort of fighting a difficult battle over an issue that doesn't affect me personally anyway? Why alienate friends and neighbors who support abortion if what they support has no real impact on our daily lives?" Little did we know then that on average well in excess of 1 million abortions would be performed annually? That's more than 30 million aborted lives since the practice was made legal—or more than one-tenth the current population of the United States. I think the tide has turned on abortion, and the amendment process would be successful.

I'm not going to pretend to be an expert on how the amendment process works or how an effort to pass an amendment should be organized. That's for others who are far more experienced than me. The amendment process is specified in the Constitution, Article V:

> The Congress, whenever two thirds of both houses shall deem it necessary, shall propose amendments to this Constitution, or, on the application of the legislatures of two thirds of the several states, shall call a convention for proposing amendments, which, in either case, shall be valid to all intents and purposes, as part of this Constitution, when ratified by the legislatures of three fourths of the several states, or by conventions in three fourths thereof, as the one or the other mode of ratification may be proposed by the Congress; provided that no amendment which may be made prior to the year one thousand eight hundred and eight shall in any manner affect the first and fourth clauses in the ninth section of the first article; and that no state, without its consent, shall be deprived of its equal suffrage in the Senate.

The process can be initiated either by the United States Congress or by the request of two-thirds of the state legislatures. Either way, any resulting amendment is then put to a vote of the people in each state. Three-fourths of the states must pass the amendment for it to be added to the Constitution. Given the current composition of the United States Congress, I think there is a better chance of initiating the amendment at the state level. This would have the added advantage of "priming" the states for the ratification vote that would come later. However, as I said earlier, I would leave that up to the experts who are well versed in how best to proceed.

As for the issue of gay marriage, I have reluctantly concluded that it should also go the constitutional amendment route. It's tempting to let individual states fight these battles by passing Defense of Marriage Acts (DOMA). Only eight states haven't passed a DOMA law, but work is underway in each of these remaining states to draft and pass such legislation. Leaving this fight to the states is a very appealing idea. Marriage has always been a state institution. It would be nice to keep it that way. However, I don't think the work going on in the states is sufficient. I think it's inevitable that the Supreme Court will eventually pass judgment on this issue. And given the past performance of the Court, I am unconvinced that it would uphold state DOMAs. As with the abortion issue, the only way to ensure that the law of the land reflects the will of the people—and not just the will of a justice or two—is to take it out of the hands of the justices. Logistically and politically, it might even be advisable to package these two amendments banning abortion and gay marriage together. Personally, I would prefer that any voting on the two occur as two separate and distinct votes, even if they are packaged together for logistical reasons. I would want each issue to stand clearly on its own merits so nobody could claim that one or the other passed only because of the overwhelming strength of its companion issue.

With gun control, I think the best we can do is align ourselves with any of a number of gun control advocacy groups and make our voices heard at the ballot box by voting for candidates who support gun control. We should also take every opportunity possible to expose the National Rifle Association for what it is: the mouthpiece of the gun industry disguised as a defender of individual rights. Unfortunately, I don't think there is much else we can do to advance this issue. Given the variety and specificity of law that would need to be constructed to limit gun ownership, it isn't a candidate for a constitutional amendment. Laws will need to be constructed to allow some guns and not others. Such laws will be complex and will require frequent modification as new weaponry becomes available. That kind of legislation just doesn't fit in the constitutional amendment process. It will take a long, persistent ground game to bring some sanity to firearm ownership in the United States. I'm sure it can be accomplished if enough of us get involved.

Finally, the issue of separation of church and state doesn't really require any specific extra-party effort. As I mentioned in the separation of church and state chapters, law is on the side of separation, and it's just a matter of time until any significant vestiges of entanglement are removed. In the meantime, it would be a good idea for those who currently are concerned about the lack of school prayer to redirect their energy to more prayer and worship at home. After all, isn't the desire for increased personal spirituality the motivation for support of school prayer? Likewise, those who attempt to keep any display of religion out of the public square ought to redirect their energy to putting their own standards on display in the public square. After all, shouldn't the public be exposed to a wide range of philosophies so each citizen can form his or her own opinion instead of having a vocal minority determine what can and cannot be experienced? And finally, those who expect government employees to check their religious beliefs at the office door ought to redirect their energy to something less silly than expecting a man or woman to be something they are not. After all, as long as government employees aren't using the power of government to advance their personal religion, their personal religion should be entirely welcome—even encouraged—as a guiding force in their public service. As much as I hope these three things would happen, I doubt they will. Wisdom will probably not prevail in the short term, but the law will certainly prevail in the long term.

In conclusion, I hope this book has challenged you to a deeper examination of your own position on each of these cultural issues and that it has motivated you to reach a solid and principled stand on each. I also hope your conclusions are consistent with mine and that you will be motivated to elect candidates and support extra-party activities that will disarm this Culture War. If I've misjudged the feelings of the silent majority, I will still be gratified to have been able to express my own opinions on these issues and hopefully have encouraged a good number of you to think more deeply and speak more freely than you would have otherwise.

978-0-595-37932-3
0-595-37932-X